Revive
Thy
Work

Revive Thy Work

WATCHMAN NEE
Translated from the Chinese

"O Lord, revive thy work . . ."
Habakkuk 3.2

Christian Fellowship Publishers, Inc.
New York

ISBN 0-935008-81-0

Available from the Publishers at:

11515 Allecingie Parkway
Richmond, Virginia 23235

PRINTED IN U.S.A.

TRANSLATOR'S PREFACE

"Revive thy work in the midst of the years" (Hab. 3.2). This was the cry of the prophet Habakkuk in view of the ruin and judgment of the nation of Judah. He pleaded with God that in wrath He would remember mercy. He was thereby shown that "the righteous shall live by his faith" (2.4): "for though the fig tree shall not flourish, neither shall fruit be on the vines; the labor of the olive shall fail, and the fields shall yield no food; the flock shall be cut off from the fold, and there shall be no herd in the stalls: yet I will rejoice in Jehovah, I will joy in the God of my salvation" (3.17-18). By faith he saw the Lord coming in His glory, going forth for the salvation of His people and of His Anointed. Hence this cry of faith!

We live in the last days. We see ruin all around, and yet with eyes of faith we can see God is working steadily towards the consummation of His eternal purpose. His work is one of recovery, restoring all the fullness of His riches in Christ which was once committed to the Church but which was lost through her unfaithfulness. By the grace given, the Church is yet to be arrayed in fine linen, the righteousness of the saints (Rev. 19.8). She is to be presented to Christ a glorious Church, holy and without blemish (Eph. 5.27). Today God is calling for the faithful to give themselves wholly to Him, to stand firmly with Him and to serve this purpose of His single-mindedly. Who will answer the call?

In 1948 brother Watchman Nee gathered with his fellow workers from all over the country of China and spent more than a month together in the city of Shanghai, waiting upon the Lord and talking about the recovery work of

God. Notes were taken by some of the attendees at these informal meetings. During these deliberations a wide range of subjects was discussed over and over again. As an aid to the reader's focus, a rearrangement of these talks has been made in the present volume according to the topics considered and not according to the dates spoken. And though the reader will notice a few instances of repetition in some aspects of the material presented from talk to talk, it was felt it would be best not to delete them since in each case God's servant was found approaching the subject at hand from a slightly different perspective, in pursuance of which he will be seen at times clarifying and enlarging further upon what was presented elsewhere. Nevertheless, to render these talks more universally applicable, all matters of *local* interest have been deleted. Generally, the topics covered in this volume are those such as the Way of Recovery, the History of Recovery, the Recovery of Body Life, the Recovery of Body Ministry, the Deliverance from Mammon, and New Testament Ministry.

Let it be our prayer that God will use these messages to revive our spirits, renew our consecration, and reinforce our commitment to the recovery work of God in this last hour.

CONTENTS

Scripture quotations are from the
American Standard Version of the Bible
(1901), unless otherwise indicated.

PART ONE

THE WAY OF RECOVERY

1 | The Way of Recovery (1)*

Concerning the way as to how to serve in this particular age, we need first of all to understand the conditions of the Church in this age. With regard to this, there are generally two different schools of thought. One school considers the Church as progressive: for in each period of Church history there has been the recovery of some special truth such as justification by faith, sanctification, and so forth. The other school, including such Brethren as John Nelson Darby, regards the Church today in a state of ruin: for, say they, if we consider the Church life of the first century in her absolute consecration and her faithful adherence to the teaching of the apostles—such as is described in Acts 2 and 4; and if we consider as well how the saints are to be perfected till the body of Christ attains to the measure of the stature of Christ's fullness as is enunciated by Paul in Ephesians 4; and if we then compare these spiritual

---

*Delivered at Workers Meeting, Shanghai, 9 April 1948. —*Translator*

phenomena and expectations of the early Church
with the actual condition of the Church today, the
difference is vast beyond the telling. Once when I
was in England, brother T. Austin-Sparks invited me
to his house for afternoon tea. In the course of our
time together he asked me my thoughts about Ephesians 4 and when I thought this would be fulfilled. I
had to acknowledge that from the human viewpoint,
the distance between today's Church and Ephesians
4 is too far apart.

From a reading of Paul's latter epistles we must
also acknowledge that the Church, even in his day,
had fallen. In 2 Timothy Paul wrote: "all that are in
Asia [Minor] turned away from me" (1.15). Peter in
his second letter outlined a similar situation. The
apostle John too declared in the end that the spirit of
the Antichrist had already come and that believers
ought to watch and to prove the spirits (see 1 John
2.18, 4.1,3).

The observations of the two opposite schools of
thought mentioned above are all factual. What God
desires today is to obtain a group of people who will
stand on His side under these two seemingly opposite states of the Church today and keep His testimony as overcomers. God has His work in each dis-
pensation. Yet His purpose throughout is to maintain
His testimony.

According to the narrative of 1 Kings, there was
no sound of hammer nor axe nor any tool of iron
heard while the temple of Solomon was being built.
This was because all the materials for the building of
the temple were either cut and measured in the

quarry or done so on the mountain before they were sent to Solomon. Every stone and each piece of wood were already perfectly matched. And hence, "there was neither hammer nor axe nor any tool of iron heard in the house, while it was in building" (6.7). In just such a manner today shall the work of God be carried out in every place around the globe.

The Book of Acts is an unfinished narrative. In the entire Bible, this is the only book without an end. The five books of Moses, the Gospel according to Matthew, the Book of Revelation, and so forth—all have a conclusion. The Book of Acts is alone different in this regard. In it one can see that many problems have not been resolved, all of them waiting for solutions. What about Paul's later works of ministry? How did these works conclude? The Book of Acts gives no clue. The reason for this lack of record is simple: it is because the Holy Spirit is still working today: in the Church today, the Holy Spirit has yet His work to do.

Submit to Authority and Accept
the Riches of the Members

The will of God today is to recover the testimony of the body of Christ. The body testimony is not a doctrine; it is a reality. In this body there is spiritual authority as well as various ministries for the perfecting of the saints. Ministry and authority are clearly related. Where there is ministry, there is authority. In Ephesians 4 we are told that the body needs gifts of all kinds to perfect the saints. For a member to be perfected, he needs to submit to authority. By submitting to authority a member is in subjection to the Head. Today the sisters wear head-covering. This is a procedure which speaks to the brothers. For in fact everyone has his or her head covered before Christ. We do not have individual heads, our head is Christ. To preserve one's own head is individualism. Whoever advocates individualism in the body is a troublemaker. Christ alone is Head. On the other hand, Christ also has His head covered before God. Though our hands and feet are quite distant from the head of our physical body, we all nonetheless know they are still under the direction of the head. For this reason, our submitting to the members of the body of Christ is today a submitting to the Lord.

Even though the mouth of our human body is important, it still is in need of the help of the other members. How helpless it would be without the assistance of the eyes and ears. True, the Bible does indeed record how people had personally received the direct grace of God and how they achieved personal holiness. Yet it also tells of our relationship with other members in the body of Christ. Is there anything today which we do not receive from others in the body? All the great heresies in the world come from what are self-proclaimed as having been direct revelations from the Lord. If a person is able to receive all revelations by himself, then he can be an individual Christian. We would have no need to assemble together. Indeed, such words in the Scriptures as "one another," "we" and "they" could all be eliminated. Not so, however, for we need to be humble and be ready to accept that which others have already received. After the first one has received, the second one finds it easier to receive from the first one. Some twenty-odd years ago it was hard for me to meet a clearly saved person. But after I had met the first saved person, it was no longer difficult for me to know saved people. This principle is applicable to all the rest of the truths.

A Normal Christian Testifies to the Body

One great revelation of the Bible concerns the will of God in His desiring all Christians to testify to the reality of the body, that is, to be members of the body of Christ. Today we need such normal or typical Christians. Who is a typical Christian? He or she is one in whom people can see certain characteristics. For example, if you are with people who belong to the Presbyterian Church, you will be told what God's predestination is and that your salvation, new birth, justification, and so forth are all preordained by God. Or, if you sit under the ministry of a Wesleyan, you will be instructed concerning your free will: you are able to repent and you must will to be saved: everything depends on you, otherwise you will not even get saved. So, among various denominational Christians, you discern certain characteristics.

Today's Christians are not normal or typical enough. They lack certain fundamental characteristics such as selling all, consecration, repentance and confession, deliverance from the power of sin, etc. When a person is newly saved you can mold him or her easily. After a long while, though, the person becomes set and fixed. Then he or she will be hard to be instructed. So we must speak to brothers and sisters as early as possible concerning these truths. How tempting it is for us to want to be popular: we desire to say pleasant words, pleasing to the ears; we try to be polite to people. And thus, we spoil their Christian life. We must therefore spend time to learn how to produce normal Christians so that the next generation of believers will be altogether new and fresh.

Experience the Reality of the Body of Christ

The body of Christ is not a theory. It is a spiritual reality. The release of something spiritually substantive is that which can be felt by people. Take as an example Evan Roberts. He released to people the truth of the kingdom. Having passed through several sicknesses, Roberts came to understand kingdom truth. When he stood up to speak, and though perhaps only for fifteen minutes, his words conveyed something real. Many had spoken on the truth of the kingdom before, but they had failed to present the substance of it. A similar circumstance surrounds the truth of the body today. Although many can talk about it, few have the substance. Before the time of J. N. Darby, many had spoken on the truth of the Church, yet they were devoid of the substance. When Darby spoke, however, it was different. He not only spoke the truth, he put the reality of the truth before men.

Does this mean that God is restricted by men? No. If God wants to work, who can limit Him? A

Christian receives much on the day of salvation. Yet gradually these riches are lost. Why? Because in his spiritual journey, the Christian picks up many other things and holds on to them tightly. Thus he has neither time nor capacity for spiritual things. Yet this is true corporately with the Church even as it is true individually with each Christian. The Letter to the Ephesians reveals the Church in her fullness. Thereafter, no one is able to reach such height.

What the believer obtains at the beginning of his Christian walk is positional gain. Henceforth it must be experiential gain. In order to gain in experience, we must suffer loss. Unless we forsake what we tightly hold, we cannot gain more experientially. One day, when we depart from this world, we may be able to say that all our loss is but gain. For this reason, today's believers need to follow God's work closely lest they become castaways.

2 | The Way of Recovery (2)*

During the Reformation the emphasis was on justification by faith. Though it was truly a recovery of an important truth, nevertheless what people saw before God was only the need for faith and not works as well. Luther indeed recovered the truth of justification by faith, but he paid attention solely to "faith," he knew little regarding the truth about "righteousness." Not till a little more than a century ago did God raise up men such as J. N. Darby to focus upon righteousness. But though they *used* the word "righteousness," they failed to touch its reality. They did not fully understand what "righteousness" is. Even so, they did teach much further on the truth of justification.

A century ago people also spoke on the truth of regeneration. But what is the relationship between regeneration and justification? Which is first and

*Delivered in Shanghai, 10 April 1948.—*Translator*

which follows are matters hard to explain. Formerly, there was a brother who preached a lot on justification and yet he never heard the truth concerning regeneration. Three years later, however, he heard this truth, and felt himself regenerated. From that day onward, whenever he went out to preach the gospel, he always told people that they must be justified before they could be regenerated. Thus he preached, and thus people at different places followed. Actually, such a clear-cut order of placing justification before regeneration is quite arbitrary.

He who has no experience is not able to preach God's truth. Yet neither can a person preach God's truth purely on the basis of experience. One who preaches God's truth must not be restricted by his own experience. He may experience certain truths in a certain order, but he should not program these truths for others according to his own experience.

Recognize the Two Sides of Truth

Truth has two sides. Many teachings only touch upon one side of truth. For example: We know the effectiveness of the cross is twofold. On the one hand it takes away our sins; on the other hand it justifies us (see 1 Peter 2.24). However, we cannot divide the cross into two parts. For in reality these are the two sides of the same thing. Through the cross we are justified from sins, and by the same cross we who have died are free from sin.

Never Circumscribe God's Word
with Personal Experience

How often we tend to circumscribe the word of
God with our own experience. Since our personal experience is partial and fragmentary, it fails to take
into account the full counsel of God's word. We usually hold to the notions that the sun comes out during
the day and that the moon appears only in the night;
and thus we say there is no moon in the daytime. Actually the moon can be seen in the day as well as in
the night. How frequently we come before God and
judge matters according to our own experience. Most
people like to arrange in a certain order the truths of
God, such as placing justification before sanctification. Who among them realizes that the Scriptures
themselves sometimes place sanctification before justification (see 1 Cor. 6.11). For in fact justification
and sanctification are the two sides of one truth. This
is why we need to be delivered from our human
weakness so as not to influence or circumscribe
God's word. We must be freed from the self that cir-
cumscribes God's word as well as from the self that
doubts His word.

Never Consider Present Understanding As Entire Truth

Do not make definitive conclusions about God's
word on the basis of the understanding of the moment. For what we see today is quite limited. It is
very possible that fifty years later brethren will rise
up to charge us as having been in darkness. May we

climb higher to view God's word accurately. Inasmuch as we are not saved before we are regenerated, so we do not obtain personal life before we know "body life." Even as salvation and regeneration are simultaneous, so the knowledge of personal and body life in Christ come at the same time. Indeed, though there is present truth (2 Peter 1.12), there is also present error. Do not allow the lack of knowledge on certain truth during a certain time to become the error of that time. For example: baptism and laying on of hands should be concurrent experiences (see Acts 9.17-18); soon after one is baptized, he should receive the laying on of hands so as to cause that person to see the Church, the body of Christ, and his having been joined to all the brothers and sisters therein. Due to the difference in the time of the recovery of these truths, people have inaccurately placed one ahead of the other. We therefore need to be careful not to conclude what we see today as being the whole truth, nor should we use our own experience as the basis for decisions we come to concerning God's word. Let us ever remember that we are the ministers of *God's* word.

Must Clearly See the Body of Christ

The oneness of the body of Christ is based on the knowledge of body life. First we recognize that the life we have is one life before we experience the oneness in this life. The lack of such knowledge is a tremendous loss for us. Let me speak frankly that one who does not see the body of Christ will never sense any difference between himself and the person who sees it. But to one who has seen the body, he will notice a great lack in the other person who does not see the body. Though an unsaved person may look upon a saved individual as being almost the same as he is, a saved person will find a huge deficiency in the unsaved one.

Concerning Practice

Having taken the first step, we can now take the second. The first step is related to the word of God; the second is related to us. First the word of God, then the outworking of His word in our lives. The first and foremost thing we each need to learn in the body of Christ is to seek to know the object of my submission. I should know who is ahead of me. Most of the authorities recorded in the Scriptures are delegated authorities, not direct authorities. What we each must learn is not who should submit to me, but to whom should I submit. For example, in the office I need not inquire who my subordinates are; rather, I need first to inquire who my boss is. If you go to work as a maid in a household, you do not need to question who are the children, but you certainly need to inquire who the master of the house is.

Now by following the movement of the inner life we will naturally find out to whom we should submit ourselves. Let us not think that submission causes uneasiness; as a matter of fact, submission gives delight. *Not* to submit is what makes one uncomfortable! Before there can be coordination in body life, there must be mutual submission. Such coordination will then be most beautiful. Yet *real* submission can only come by the operation of the *inner life* and not by any *external* cause. It is not right nor spiritual if submission is given purely because of higher position or more wealth. For that is how the world obtains submission. No, our submission should be the result of the demand of the inner life, not the requirement of outward causes.

Such submission may indeed cause us to shed tears; nevertheless, there is rejoicing in our hearts. Though distressed, yet we are gladdened by having done it. Sometimes the object of our submission may give us troubles; even so, we still can say, Amen. This is genuine submission.

Fellowship and Coordination

If we see the body of Christ, we will also see fellowship. The Head gives us life that we may be meek and tender in being coordinated together. In such coordination, we will not rub against one another nor will we murmur against each other. Where is our difference from the world if such conflict and murmurs exist in the body of Christ?

In the Scriptures many words of the Lord are not spoken directly to the person in question. We see, for instance, that after the Lord met Saul He did not reveal His will to Saul directly; rather, the Lord sent Ananias to speak the word to him (see Acts 9.6,17). In one sense the life of the New Covenant is intensely personal; in another sense, however, the First

Epistle of John mentions this: "that ye also may have fellowship with us" (1.3). So, this fellowship is a sharing with one another. On one side, we individually pass through the veil to come before God by the precious blood (Heb. 10.19-20). On the other side, we work together, walk together, and coordinate together in our service. Here we serve and are being served. From reading the Biblical narratives concerning Paul, Luke, Timothy and others, we learn there is coordination among them. When Paul relates something, all say it is good and proceed immediately to carry the matter forward (see Acts 16.9-10). Timothy is a good brother. Had he wanted to, he could have written to Paul, saying, "Brother Paul, I have believed in the Lord for many years. I know how to pray and how to seek the Lord. Will you please give me some liberty?" But Timothy has not done that. This is because, though each one comes to God individually and is personally responsible to God, yet no one can be independent or completely free. Whether you are joined to one another or not, you nonetheless know it in your heart. There is no need to be told.

out of the overflow of the heart the mouth speaks
Mt. 12

Be Delivered from Self

The mouth can certainly talk, but a man's mouth may not necessarily represent his personality. Sometimes he may approve with his mouth yet oppose in his heart. Some brothers and sisters come to the meeting bringing with them their mouths but not themselves. One day a sister came to me to discuss the matter of submission in the family. She said she wanted me to help. But I knew clearly in my heart that her mouth and her ears had come but she herself was absent. When a person sets aside his personal opinion, he knows within what is right though his mouth may not wish to confess it.

We need to learn to be delivered from self. Suppose fifty radios are tuned in to the same radio station, and yet my radio—one of the fifty—receives a different signal from that of the others. It is obvious that something is wrong with *my* radio. Although according to the New Covenant we all have the Lord in us, nonetheless we also are in the Church, the body of Christ. Thus we need to be joined practically to other members. In body coordination, we must pay attention to the feeling of the other members. Only then can we have good coordination.

The human body is the most beautiful thing in the entire world, but it may become the ugliest of all. A man standing there is something beautiful to behold. Yet if I later pass by and see only one isolated member of that man's body standing there, I will reckon it as most repulsive. Suppose I enter a house and see two legs at the door, a pair of ears in the room, and two arms on the stairway. How horrible this would be! I would immediately flee from the scene! Similarly, a person who acts independently outside the body of Christ creates a most dreadful scene. To confess being in the body and to be coordinated in the body are two distinct things. Independent action is most unbecoming.

Submit to the Ministerial Authority

Authority is related to the Head of the Church. It also is related to ministry. Please remember that all the members in the body of Christ each have their special gift. Whether ears, eyes, mouth, hands, feet, or whatever—each has his gift. And these gifts constitute their ministries (see 1 Cor. 12.4-12). Moreover, where there is ministry, there is authority. Why is this so? Because each receives a different ministry and a different ministry produces a particular authority. On the other hand, though, because of the authority inherent in ministry, there is restriction. For instance, if God gives me peace in making me an ear that I may hear, He in one sense wants me to serve the body of Christ with my hearing but in another sense wishes me to accept my limitation. For if I desire to see, I must receive the help of the eye. The problem today lies in the fact that that which cannot hear craves to hear, that which cannot speak longs to speak, and that which cannot run aspires to run. Yet one should understand that what the others in the body have done actually means his having done also since their gifts are also his (see 1 Cor. 3.21). We all need to learn the lesson of limitation because the Church is a body.

Someone may not be called to be a Bible teacher. Yet if he insists on teaching the Bible, he will cause trouble. Should the Lord grace you to be a hand, it is quite right for you to lift your hand high. But suppose you declare you can also see; then you will never succeed even if you should try to see for a lifetime. Let your and my prayer be, "O Lord, cause me to see my limitation." For if you have *all* the gifts, you will be the body. To accept limitation is the greatest test in the principle of body coordination. He who knows limitation will in all things seek for fellowship, and also seek help.

Let us realize that authority is inherent in ministry. The ear has the ministry of hearing; therefore, it has the authority of hearing. Unless you see your limitation you will not be able to submit to authority, however hard you may try. For only those who see their limitation can be joined to the other members in the body of Christ.

Some brother considers himself capable of expounding the Scriptures. So he sets himself up as a Bible expositor. He insists on teaching though he is not thus gifted; consequently, he brings in strange doctrine.

Many do not understand what Paul meant when he wrote: "all things are yours" (1 Cor. 3.21). Let us realize that we are born into a very rich family. We ought therefore to be glad because we are so rich in the Lord. Our inner feeling should induce us to accept authority. Our inner man should always yield to ministerial authority. On the one hand we ought to see our limitation and on the other hand we ought to see that all authorities have been set up by the Lord. The ability the Lord gives to a person constitutes that person's authority.

To Submit to Ministry Is to Submit to God

As you learn to submit to ministry, you actually

are submitting to God. You cannot insist that you
only want to obey God directly. For the authorities
which God has established in this world are ninety-
nine percent *delegated* authorities. The Scriptures
mention subjection to husbands, to government, to
the elderly, and so forth. Apart from a few particular
places in the Bible, all the rest of the Scriptures refer
to delegated authority. He who is not able to be subject to delegated authority cannot be in subjection to
God. Though the human eye can see, it is actually
under the direction of the head. What you meet is
the eye, yet behind the eye is the head. Just so, in the
body of Christ, if you are able to see the Head behind the eye, it will not be difficult for you to yield.

Christ's teaching on the mount as recorded in the
Gospel of Matthew is not meant for our distress, but
rather for our comfort. To walk the first mile is
doubtless distressing, but the second mile gives joy
(5.41). The "Blessed" repeatedly found in Matthew
5.3-12 should be translated "Happy." Submission is a
joyful experience, for the life the Lord gives us is a
happy one. The Head confers ministry. Where there
is ministry, there is also authority. We sense joy and
comfort when we yield to authority.

In service we should see who is ahead of us and
find opportunity to submit. I do not believe there can
be a single brother who is not under another brother.
The very nature of the life within you demands that
you find the one to whom to submit. Sisters cover
their heads not by their natural hairs but by a covering. The very act of the wearing of a covering is an
expression of one's seeking to submit. Why do we not

pursue submission as we pursue love and knowledge? Why do we not pay as much attention to submission as to work? Why do we not take delight in obedience as we do in preaching the gospel? In the local church we ought to learn to be under the authority of one or more. May I reiterate that if there is no ministry there is no authority. But where ministry is, there is authority.

In the local church there is positional authority as well as spiritual authority. Paul sent out Titus and Timothy to appoint elders. These elders, once appointed, automatically have positional authority. If you, having lacked spiritual discernment, set up three elders and three years later you discover four other men who are more spiritually advanced than these three, what can you do? Will you change the old for the new? Or ask the old to retire? We should respect God's appointed authority according to the will of the Lord.

I want to testify that God has His arrangements in the Church. If you submit yourself to these arrangements, you will be profited. Ministry is authority. As you subject yourself to the authority of such ministry, you will be edified. There was one sister who used to act as head of her family. For the sake of subjecting herself to her husband, she came to see me. She told me she could not submit to her husband because he was unable to make any decision nor did he have any opinion. My answer was: "You just submit, just ask him for all things. He will not *every* time be able to say he does not know. By this means you will ultimately force him to seek God. So, you must learn how to be pious and to fear God. Your submission does not degrade you. Quite the contrary, your submission will help your husband. For God has appointed you to be a submissive person. Your submission will help other people, especially your husband." We are not chosen without a reason. We are chosen for the sake of submission.

Paul could boldly proclaim, "My gospel" (Rom. 2.16, 16.25). He also told Timothy: "abide thou in the things which thou hast learned . . ., knowing of whom thou hast learned them" (2 Tim. 3.14). This is because he is a bona fide apostle. With his manifold ministry and gift, he has the authority to remind people of his gospel, his ministry and his teaching.

A person, as led by the life of Christ within him, should put himself under two or three people and learn to submit to them. This is not only profitable to himself but also to the local church. A member in the body of Christ is like a stone in the holy temple of old. The Jewish temple had been built with fitly framed stones. To build is to have a stone suitably placed upon another; ruin, on the other hand, is to have no stone upon any other.

The Course before Us Today

The Lord is always going forward. What we considered as life yesterday may become spiritual death for us today. We must go forward and not remain in past experience. We believe what the Lord does today is far more abundant than before. All who have their eyes opened can see that today is the rich-

est of all days. Such riches are accumulated in the
time of ruin. On the one hand, the Church is progressive and advancing; on the other hand, she is lin-
gering in an age of ruin. Some see only the ruin of
the Church without seeing her advance as well. Yet
some see the advance of the Church without seeing
her ruin. We need to see both. Viewing from the perspective of what the Lord is doing today, we may say
the Lord is always advancing. But as we look around
us, we can also say that the Church is in ruin.

What God is doing today is raising up the testimony of the local church in the day of ruin, using the
local church to respond to God's call in the day of
the ruin of the Church, and through such testimony
to recover the Church from her ruin. Christianity
today has departed from the truth and has fallen into
ruin. For this reason, today's Christians are not normal, they are falling short of God's standard. A typical Christian must not only be a normal Christian
personally but also bear the testimony of the local
church. With such testimony may the Church be
brought out from her ruinous condition and be
brought into an abundant sphere.

"My Father worketh even until now, and I work,"
said the Lord (John 5.17). The Father is always working. He never ceases working. Hence, we too must
work. Our work today is to obtain for the Lord the
testimony of the local church. Our ministry today is
that of the Church, that is, the ministry of obtaining
for the Lord the testimony of the local church.

True, the state of the Church today is ruinous. Typologically speaking, the Church has been taken into

Babylonian captivity. What Paul witnessed of the glory of the Church in the first century faded away quickly. Since then the Church has fallen into a state of captivity. This continued on to the age of Thyatira. After Thyatira there was Sardis when God began to do the work of recovery (see Rev. 2.18, 3.1). Thyatira represents the Roman Catholic Church; and Sardis, the Protestant Church. But beginning from Sardis, God commenced His recovery work. Although various truths had been lost over a prolonged period of time, they became more real when they were recovered. In the first century when Paul spoke on these truths they had some spiritual reality, though they were not sufficiently real. For example, though the Church he spoke about was a reality to him, nevertheless at that time the glorious Church had yet to appear. After the Reformation, not only these truths themselves were recovered, the actual things of which these truths spoke were also restored. For example, in the matter of justification by faith, it became an actual *experience* as well as a recovered *truth*. If the Lord delays His return, the Church will never be able to induce people to be justified by works—simply because the actual reality called justification by faith has long since been restored to the Church.

What the Church needs today is the raising up of the ministry of maintaining the testimony of the Lord. The problem in many places today lies in the fact that there is the presence of the local church without there being the ministry of maintaining the Lord's testimony. Today's ministry therefore needs to be elevated to the level at which God is working. We may have a so-called ministry, but we need more urgently a ministry for the testimony. The ministry must be a ministry of the church, a ministry of the testimony of the church.

God's present ministry is in the local church and is also for the local church. What ministry does is to recover the testimony the church ought to have. This alone is true recovery. Ministry is for testimony.

The present time is not an ordinary time. Our present work is not an ordinary work. Today's way is the way of the Church. We cannot afford to run wildly in this way of the Church by doing whatever pleases us. For this will hinder the forward march of the Lord. The concept of the body in 1 Corinthians 12 is the assigned testimony of the local church. It is the testimony of the body—that is, of body life. In this body, "the eye cannot say to the hand, I have no need of thee: nor again the head to the feet, I have no need of you" (v.21). All members of the body of Christ must be coordinated. Ephesians 4 reveals to us the reality of the relationship between the body and the Head. The local church today should demonstrate the testimony of this body reality. It is to show forth in the locality the reality of the body.

3 | The Way of Recovery (3)*

Old Testament Typology: Tabernacle and Temple Typify Two Sides of the Church

Concerning this matter of the ruin of the Church, let us first observe the path the Church follows on earth. The path she travels on earth is like that of the tabernacle in the Old Testament. The tabernacle was instituted by God. Its purpose was for God to dwell among the children of Israel (Ex. 25.8). God at first dwelt in the tabernacle; then, after the temple was built He also dwelt in it (see 1 Kings 9.3,7). Hence both the tabernacle and the temple are types of God dwelling among men. These two may appear typologically similar, but actually they are not. In the past, many books have been written on the typology of the tabernacle, but few are the books written on that of the temple. Though both represent the Church, there

---

*Delivered at Workers Meeting, Shanghai, 11 April 1948.
—*Translator*

are nonetheless some fundamental differences between the two.

The tabernacle was made in the wilderness under the direction of Moses and Aaron. The temple was built in Jerusalem, prepared by David and constructed by Solomon. The tabernacle had coverings and curtains but no floor. As people entered the tabernacle the ground under their feet was the sand. This immediately reminded them that the tabernacle was not permanent but movable. And that is why it was called the "tabernacle," or *tent* of meeting.

The temple did have many features similar to the tabernacle. In the latter there were gold, silver and brass; but so were these metals in the temple. In the tabernacle, there was wood; the same was found in the temple. However, the temple had stones which the tabernacle did not have; and stones were its conspicuous building material. There were no stones in the tabernacle for stones represent stability; they are not easily moved. The tabernacle was instituted for the wilderness, the latter being the Israelites' temporal dwelling place; the temple, on the other hand, was set up for the kingdom, Israel's permanent place of abode. David represents the Lord; and Solomon, the Holy Spirit. The very name of Solomon means "peaceful"; and hence, God sent the Spirit of peace to build the temple. So David typifies the Incarnated Christ while Solomon typifies the Holy Spirit.

And thus in Scripture there are two presentations of the dwelling place of God. One is on earth, temporary and mobile, as typified by the tabernacle. The tabernacle moved around: at one time it was at Elim;

at another time at Kadesh-Barnea: sometimes it was pitched in land of abundant supply; sometimes, in land of bitter water. Yet the tabernacle remained intact. Whenever the children of Israel encamped, the tabernacle was always there. Hence the tabernacle represents God's Church on earth, that is, the local church. In Shanghai, the church is there because God's people are there. Wherever the people of God gather, there is the church. But if they are scattered to different places, then the church disappears. Such is the tabernacle aspect of the Church.

The temple, though, was different from the tabernacle. It was erected on Ornan's threshing floor (2 Chron. 3.1) and was built with stones. It was established for the Jewish kingdom. It was the center of the new life of the children of Israel. The temple was one: permanent and strong and undivided. The political situation might cause division, but the temple could not be divided. There could only be one temple.

Thus we see that on the one hand the Church can appear at various places, but on the other hand the spiritual reality of the Church is one body, united and eternal. Such are the two pictures of the Church as represented by the tabernacle and temple of old.

The visible Church we see today is in type the tabernacle that is already in ruin, with the temple having not yet been manifested. From heaven's viewpoint the Church mentioned in Ephesians 2 as being "a habitation of God in the Spirit" is indeed a fact (vv.21-22). But in performance the Church is still in the process of fulfillment. She has not yet wholly appeared. When in 1925 we related the history of the ark we had noted that the ark was always in the process of advancing. It first crossed the River Jordan, then it rested in Shiloh (Josh. 18.1). During the battle which then ensued between the children of Israel and the Philistines, the two sons of Eli sinned, and God's priest Eli himself had become dull and weak. He knew why the children of Israel were defeated, and yet he agreed to let the ark go into the battle, hoping that by its presence Israel might still somehow win. The children of Israel were nonetheless defeated, and the ark was taken captive by the Philistines and brought into the house of their god Dagon. God sent a plague upon the Philistines who eventually sent the ark back to the Israelites, but transported it on an ox-cart (see 1 Sam. 4-6).

At that time Samuel entered into priestly ministry. He, being a child, was girded with a linen ephod (1 Sam. 2.18). Here in type is a ministry that prepares for the Kingdom. The ark represents Christ. Where the ark is, there is the presence of the Lord. It should be noted that the ark was also sometimes called the ark of the testimony for at that time it was the center of God's testimony. Without the ark, the tabernacle was an empty tent. With the ark, the tabernacle became most meaningful. Now from the moment the ark left the tabernacle in Shiloh and was captured (4.17), from that time forth it never again returned to the tabernacle. It wandered around till it was received into the temple after the latter was built (1 Kings 8.1-21). Before David, there was Saul. During that period, Shiloh was forsaken by God. Instead of returning to the tabernacle the ark abode in the

house of Abinidab on the hill (1 Sam. 7.1). After
David came to the throne he ultimately brought the
ark to Jerusalem to the tent which he had prepared
for it (2 Sam. 6.17). At his first attempt to do so,
however, he failed because he had adopted the way
of the Philistines in transporting the ark on an ox-
cart. Moreover, at the threshing-floor of Nacon,
Uzzah put forth his hand to the ark of God and took
hold of it, for the oxen had stumbled. But God smote
him to death. Immediately David grew afraid and
carried the ark aside into the house of Obed-edom.
Three months later, he properly brought the ark into
Jerusalem with joy; for this time the ark was carried
on the shoulders of the priests according to the ordinance of God (see 2 Sam. 6).

Jeremiah 7, verses 12 and 14 mention how God
dealt with Shiloh. Psalm 78.60-1 and 1 Samuel 4.3-4
tell how the ark left the tabernacle. And 2 Chronicles
5 narrates how the ark ultimately found its way into
the temple. The way God dealt with Shiloh was not
by consuming the land with fire or by destroying the
inhabitants there, but by removing the ark from
Shiloh. The tabernacle remained, but the ark was
now gone. This was judgment, punishment and ruin.
Just as Shiloh had only the external structure of the
tabernacle devoid of the presence of the ark, so
Christianity is today; for she has the name of the
Church, but the central testimony of the Church has
been lost. The testimony of God no longer exists.

When Solomon ascended the throne, he went to
Gibeon and there in the tabernacle (it had been
moved to here from elsewhere—cf. 1 Chron. 16.39; 2

Chron. 1.3) he asked for wisdom. But after he received wisdom, he returned to the ark (1 Kings 3.15). Now according to the tenor of 1 Kings 3.4 and 2 Chronicles 1.3, it would appear that the children of Israel had the habit of going to Gibeon to offer sacrifices at the tabernacle and to inquire of God. But Solomon, after he departed from the tabernacle that day, never again went to it. Though in Gibeon there was still the appearance of worship, yet all who received wisdom would not frequent the tabernacle anymore. For they had all begun to follow the ark.

The New Testament Situation

The Church on earth is one. Under normal condition all who are in the Church have been separated from the world. Moreover, every brother and sister is occupied with serving God. Each and every one is a consecrated person. They share all things. Also under such normal condition, the ministries according to grace are manifested such as are mentioned in Ephesians 4: there are apostles, prophets, evangelists, and shepherds and teachers. Though God's people are scattered in various places, they all are in the one Church. It can be likened to the one and same electric current that flows to many places. Although the lights which shine in different houses may differ in strength, the electricity itself is one and the same. Though the lights it lights up in various places may be different, the source remains the same. So is it in the Church. In spite of the variety of localities, the Church itself is one Church. So the Church on earth is to testify to its oneness. When we mention "local church," the emphasis is on the church, not on locality. The life in all these local churches is one life. Hence there should be a oneness among the local churches. The church may appear in Corinth, in Ephesus and in other places, but these churches are one Church. This is the normal state.

With the Church's fall into ruin, however, her condition had changed drastically. At the time of Paul, even, the Church had already commenced its ruin. In his Letter to the Philippians he wrote, "they all seek their own, not the things of Jesus Christ" (2.21). In his 2 Timothy letter he also wrote this: "all that are in Asia [Minor] turned away from me" (1.15). The letters of Peter are no exception. He too made mention of the ruinous condition of the Church in latter days. In his First Letter he spoke of the Church as a spiritual house, which is a spiritual temple (2.5); but by the time of his Second Letter he was describing all sorts of ruinous conditions. The letters of John mentioned as well the coming of the Antichrist and of apostasy (1 John 2.18, 4.3; 2 John 7). These are the phenomena of the last days. In Revelation chapters 2 and 3 one can discern that the Church had so entered into such ruinous situations already that the Risen and Ascended Lord could not write to the local churches cited but to the messengers of these churches instead. In fact, the letter of the Lord to the church in Ephesus found in Revelation 2 may be taken as the *second* letter to the Ephesians. There the church had left its first love of Paul's day and had drifted farther and farther away.

What we see today is a host of new methods, teachings, ideas and criticisms. Amidst the ruin of the Church we need to learn to judge. No doubt about it, in the denominational churches there are people who worship God. We have to acknowledge that there are also sacrifices. But the ark has already left: the testimony is lost; only the external appearance of the tabernacle remains; for as at the time of the ruin of the tabernacle of old, the eyes of God must turn to the temple. Today all who learn to follow the Lord must choose their way between the tabernacle and the temple. Some opt for that which is visible and established, for these are more tangible. Yet those who follow God choose to follow the ark— wheresoever it goes.

The ground we ought to stand on is a spiritual ground, which is represented by the temple. Today the Church is the habitation of the Holy Spirit. In the Church there are the authority and the will of God. There is also the authority of the kingdom of the heavens. The Lord has given that authority to the Church. In the Church today we may enjoy something of the powers of the age to come (see Heb. 6.5). In the Old Testament period the temple and the kingdom were joined together. The temple was the greatest thing in the kingdom. Likewise, the Church as the temple is related to the power of the coming kingdom. Therefore, our way lies here. On the one hand, we will depart from the external tabernacle; on the other hand, we must seek after the place where God's testimony is. God has already clearly judged the external failure by removing the ark. Before God, the absence of the ark is a shame. For this reason, we must leave the tabernacle and seek after God's testimony.

What is the testimony of God? In the Old Testament time God had ordered Moses to prepare two stone tablets on which were inscribed the Ten Commandments. These tablets were called the tables of law. They were also called the tables of the testimony. God also commanded to have an ark built. That ark represents Christ. Now on the ark was the mercy seat; and in the ark was the law—the two stone tablets. Yet God did not call the ark the ark of the law; rather, He called it the ark of the testimony (Ex. 25.22). So the law is the testimony of God.

The law is God's demand on men's conduct. How does it become God's testimony? Let us understand that while God's testimony is the satisfaction of His demand on men, His demand is the testimony itself. Where there is divine demand, there is divine testimony. Whatsoever God demands of men, there the law declares God's demand; the mercy seat, though, illustrates God's grace. Testimony goes back to God, and peace comes towards men. When the glory finds its satisfaction, then there is the mercy seat. Let us realize that the Ten Commandments do not speak of dead law; they elucidate God's living demand on men. Such demand is a testimony, for God is testifying in himself. The law maintains the testimony of God. It also testifies of God. For God needs to explain His demands to men; and such explanation is the testimony of God. Psalm 119 frequently treats God's law as testimonies. Keeping God's law is therefore keeping God's testimonies. Each time Psalm 119 mentions testimonies it refers to the law.

Today the visible Church is weak and has failed. It has lost the testimony of God. It has not maintained God's demand. There are disunity, divisions, sects, parties, and so forth. What God demands, men fail to respond to in obedience. Thus, the testimony is lost and divisions are produced. With the rising up of the revivalists, still more tents are being established; but within these tents there is not the ark of the testimony. Even if there be a mercy seat, there is no ark. People may conduct revival meetings from place to place, that is to say, moving their tents here and there; yet what they maintain is but a mercy seat void of the ark. Though the mercy seat is indeed set forth, there is no testimony. This is what men are doing today: substituting the need of men for the testimony of God. Whenever men's need is substituted for God's testimony, the fall begins. Where, then, lies the way for us?

Today's Way to Work

God has His specific demand. He demands that we learn mutual dependency and coordination. He not merely requires us to be delivered from sin, the world and the flesh; He even more so calls us to come out of our individualism. In this matter of knowing the body of Christ, the Christian's difficulty lies in the fact that from the very first day of his regeneration he receives the wrong instruction. Ever since the Reformation there has been the common notion that man may be a Christian independently. He may be sanctified, justified and serve God all by himself. Such a perception by the Christian is wrong from the very outset. And thus, the way he travels thereafter is necessarily wrong. How incorrect it is for people to think that as soon as one believes in the Lord, so long as he is zealous, consecrated and forsakes all, that is enough.

If we lay a good foundation today, the situation will be greatly changed twenty or thirty years later. We need to see that one cannot be a Christian independently. He needs to follow the footsteps of the flock. He must not embrace individualism. As soon as he is baptized, he should immediately be instructed that he needs to be joined to the body of Christ. The meaning of the laying on of hands is a being joined to Christ's body—the Church. After a new believer receives the laying on of hands, he is joined to the body in local expression and is delivered from being an independent Christian.

We must acknowledge our personal limitation and therefore our need for mutual dependency. Such need is easy for young people to perceive and accept, but hard for those richly gifted to acknowledge. Nonetheless, we all must realize that however great is the function of the hands and the feet in the body, they are but hands and feet. They cannot be complete without receiving from the other members. How we must confess our limitation! The problem in the Church is caused by people considering themselves as all-round individuals. They want to do everything by their own selves. The fact of the matter is that a hand can only be a hand since it can neither see nor hear. It has to accept the seeing and hearing of other members if it is to be complete. Notwithstanding the greatness of a person's gift, he is still in need of the supply of others in many areas. As a member, he will need others' help. Yet it is more than a matter of asking for help; it is in addition a fundamental acknowledgment of one's own limitation. The hand must confess that it can neither see nor hear nor speak.

We should definitely realize our personal limitation. In case we ourselves fail to recognize our limitation, there will be others in the Church who know our bounds. For what we cannot do, other people can. Let us not think that we need only preach the Head and not the body as well. The more we depend on the Lord, the more we sense the need of the members. Unless we accept our limitation, we will never find the way. So long as this matter of our own limitation remains unacknowledged, we can make no progress. For what we have individually is so little. Let us not consider ourselves to be so mighty and wise that others may err but we ourselves never. Let us be delivered from pride and individualism. Let us be humble enough to accept another's supply. All who are habitually wise and unerring need to return and be changed. This is the first consideration in knowing and realizing the way ahead for us.

Another issue to be considered is to know submission. In the body of Christ, ministry is authority. Whoever is able to hear or to speak has authority. For example, a certain member can see; and this is the basis for his authority. His ability is his authority. Then, too, another member can hear. And his ability to hear constitutes his authority. Anyone desiring to hear must submit to him. And if anyone wants to see, he must submit to the eye. In the Church there is no one who does not need to submit to others whom God has sovereignly arranged to be there. Today's difficulty with many believers lies in the false concept they have that they must receive everything directly from God because what comes from brothers and sisters is not effectual. They reject everything which is delivered by men. But the command of God often comes through His ministries. Therefore, all must learn to submit to those who bear these ministries.

A minister ought not to speak casually. He should never expect people to submit to his authority while he himself refuses the discipline of God upon his own life. God could never commit anything to such a person. God will only commit His authority to the one who through discipline has no taste for meddling in another's freedom.

Being in the body of Christ, no member should take pleasure in hurting another member. A person who has been disciplined by God will first of all be delivered from the lust of tampering with another's freedom of choice. And secondly, the disciplined one loves to be taught concerning his own way with God. A beautiful body life appears when all the hundreds of members are joined together, with every member abstaining from meddling but ready always to be taught. Such is the balanced life in the body.

Let us be teachable and resist individualism. Let

us accept limitation on the one hand and learn to be submissive on the other. Seeking submission should be a joyful thing. Today in the world, be it nation or society, it is full of opinions, voices, protests, controversies and so forth. Because of this, every group has its bylaws. At a conference, for example, whoever asks questions or gives answers is limited to three minutes. This illustrates the fact that even in the world the individual must accept group restriction, although such restriction is man-made and outside the realm of spiritual submission.

Man's first sin was rebellion, lawlessness and resisting authority. Satan's fall and rebellion was due to his lifting up himself above God. Today, whoever is in subjection to authority bears a good testimony. May we see that not everyone has the same authority or has the word of God. Today the body testimony depends not on the number of people but on whether members can submit to God's order or whether they want to follow their own opinion. For us to be members of the body we must in all things not follow our own opinion. Rich is the deposit of Christ in the Church today. If we can stand on the receiving ground, how very rich we will be! If, though, we are only willing to receive from God directly and unwilling to receive from the body, then we will become very poor indeed. This is not just a teaching, this is a fact. Let us understand that not only what *I* have is mine: what the brothers and sisters have is also mine. In certain matters the brothers and sisters see more clearly than I do. I must therefore accept their view. Some people know the mind of God; others can clearly define truth; and so, I love to accept that which they understand and suggest: what I do not know, somebody else will know. Should we refuse to receive from others, then even after fifty years we shall have very little.

Hence, today we would beg brothers and sisters to receive from others. If they do, such will be wonderful. Yet if people should confess on the one hand that they are poor and weak but refuse on the other hand to receive riches from others, will this not be strange? How rich are the ministries which God has raised up in the Church, and yet we are still in hunger! The reason lies in our over-valuation of individualism. We should learn to bow our heads and receive supply from others.

To have the laying on of hands is the symbol of one's willingness to accept the judgment of the Church, of one's readiness to submit to the authority that God has arranged for him (see Acts 13.2-3). In Old Testament times people laid their hands on the head of the lamb to show that they were willing to hand over the lamb to be sacrificed to God. Whoever wanted to keep the lamb would therefore not lay hands on it. The Bible suggests that man ought to come to the altar and hand over the sacrifice with gladness (see 2 Cor. 9.7). Today God wants us to hand ourselves over to Him. The Book of Acts records the laying on of hands as well as baptism. The laying on of hands signifies the acceptance of the authority of the Church. On the one hand people can see in baptism how believers are delivered from the world system, but on the other hand they fail to see

the laying on of hands as constituting the acceptance
of the authority that God sets in the Church. Because
brethren refuse to accept authority, confusion results. How easy it would be to serve if all were willing
to hand themselves over to God.

The Principle of Work

This same principle of which we have been speaking applies to the work of God. All fellow workers
should first put themselves under the headship of
Christ. Only when workers accept the rule of the
Head is the Lord able to work. They should then put
themselves in the body and accept its judgment. Thus
will there be life, power and the way of God today.
Otherwise there will be rebellion and insubordination. The final manifestation of the body of Christ re-
lies on the testimony of the local churches today. In
today's local church is to be found in miniature the
future Universal Church. It is similar in situation to
the small model which an architect constructs in an-
ticipation of the future house to be built. Though the
model is not so big, in essence it is the same as the
future house to be built. 1 Corinthians 12 speaks of
the Universal Church on the one hand and of body
life in the local church on the other.

In the work of God we need to find a sure way.
What we lack today is not just power. We lack the
way—God's way. The workers are not fully committed to the Lord and to one another. Although there
is a little power, it is not powerful enough. Though a
three-dimensional cup can contain much water, a

broken glass or a two-dimensional plate cannot retain water. Today much of God's work is carried
forth on a flat surface, and therefore many blessings
leak away. Both the tabernacle and the temple in the
Old Testament period typify the New Testament
Church, which is the body of Christ. This body is
cubic, as it were, and hence it can be God's vessel for
the storage of His riches and the manifestation of a
strong testimony.

Not the workers alone, but all the brothers and
sisters must wholly consecrate themselves. In whatever circumstance they may be, they are all serving
God. Each one of His workers should count the cost
and commit himself to the Head and to His body.

The gospel is preached from Jerusalem, then to
Judea and Samaria, and finally to the ends of the
earth. This is God's way. It is wrong to commence
from the ends of the earth. It has to be from the center to the circumference. Yet for the believers to remain in Jerusalem is also wrong because the heart desire of the Lord is to the ends of the earth. For this
reason, He uses persecution to send His followers out.

PART TWO

THE HISTORY OF RECOVERY

1 | Commencement and Continuance of Recovery*

Commencement of Recovery—Martin Luther

God's recovery began with Martin Luther. This is not to say that in Luther alone was there recovery, for at that time there were other people who had the same insight. Nevertheless, he appears to stand as the representative of that period of recovery. By that time truth had become tradition and apostolic ministry had turned into papal authority. Moreover, the unity of the Church had degenerated into a Church federation, while spiritual authority had transformed itself into political power. In short, the Church had been taken into Babylonian captivity.

The human concept during that age had come to be understood as the Church controlling the world. Indeed, the Church declared that the entire world belonged to God. As a consequence, the Roman Catholic Church now brought the unsaved into the Church. All Roman citizens automatically became

---

*Delivered at Hardoon Road, Shanghai, 12 April 1948. —*Translator*

members of the Church. Naturally, therefore, the rite
of infant baptism was created. But there was yet another development which resulted from the marriage
between the Church and the world. Formerly, Christians had been a company of saints that practiced
voluntary poverty. The poor and the Christians were
one. After the Church brought in the world, however, voluntary poverty vanished: the Church had become rich. In the Church there should be only two
classes of people—both of them poor: the *naturally*
poor, and the *voluntarily* poor. Nonetheless, by the
time of Luther and even earlier, the Church had only
the first class of the poor, the second class having
well-nigh disappeared from the scene: apart from the
naturally poor the Church was now well populated
with the rich. Yet, though these latter folk were rich
in wealth, they were poor in faith.

The sad consequence of all this was that there
were fewer and fewer spiritual riches in the Church.

The Recovery of Voluntary Poverty

From the time of Clement, truths gradually grew
dim. People could analyze and expound, but spiritual
life was missing. There was no grace and very little
righteousness. Even during the days of Augustine,
truths were very unclear. In its history the Church
continued to fall further and further till a reaction
appeared in the Roman Catholic Church. Francis of
Assisi, himself a Catholic, was one of those who re-
acted. He was dissatisfied with the outward riches of
the Church. He himself was a man of wealth, at least

he was the son of a rich man. But soon he sold all that was his and gave to the poor. Thereafter he began to live a life of voluntary poverty. Though we can hardly approve of all his writings, his practice of voluntary poverty was right.

In the Church the principle to be followed should be: "He that gathered much had nothing over; and he that gathered little had no lack" (2 Cor. 8.15). To gather much is not sin, but to gather much and have bounty left over *is* sin. A person who knows the Lord will invest in the Lord. If he says he loves the Lord and yet refuses to invest in Him, his love is false. The Lord Jesus once said, "The poor ye have always with you" (John 12.8). Yet please note that He did not say that there would always be poor brothers in the Church. What He said was that the poor would always be with us. It is not a difficult matter to solve the lack among the Christian brethren. For if the brethren will give away their bounty, the poor in the Church will disappear. To *retain* is not the principle of the Lord; to *give* is His principle. If we should all give, then there shall not be any unwanted wealth. It is an abnormal phenomenon to have too rich a people in the Church. What is left over should be given away. The world loves money more than life. But God demands our lives. No Christian can afford to be careless in this area. God is careful to have our lives far much more than to have our wealth.

Much later after Francis, God raised up Count von Zinzendorf in Saxony, Germany. He belonged to the nobility and was highly educated. For the Lord's sake he opened his estate in the early eighteenth century to receive the saints from Bohemia, Moravia and other lands—especially those who were being persecuted. Through him, in fact, the Moravian Church was revived after nearly being exterminated a century before. And from that Church more men and women would be sent out as missionaries than from any of the other Churches. Indeed, the ratio of Moravian missionaries to total Church membership was even higher than could be found among the other Church organizations. Still later there was Sister Eva. She was a German. She too chose the way of voluntary poverty.

A century ago the Brethren of Great Britain were raised up. They were strong in truth but also strong in another area. Though they were hesitant in telling about themselves, many leaders among them sold all they had and followed the Lord. This issue of money and wealth must be resolved in the life of the Christian. The Lord will have no outlet if this area is unresolved among Christians. Wherein does the Church fall? It falls when the worldly principle of economics seeps into the Church. For wherever that principle is operative, everything comes under the scrutiny of cost. And thus, the Lord's way is blocked.

Deficiency of the Reformation

In Luther we see the recovery of faith. He is not very clear on righteousness. History tells us that he chastised and beat himself in order to be justified before God. In Rome on one occasion he even climbed on his knees the entire lengthy set of stairsteps of what was called Pilate's Staircase—so that he might be justified. Ultimately Luther was shown that man is not justified by works but rather by faith.

True, Luther came out of Babylon, but he failed to enter Jerusalem. He brought in the power of politics to help the protesting or Protestant Church, not realizing that such political power would in the end damage the Church instead of help her. The result from Luther's action was the creation of the national church that in essence was the unequal yoking together of politics and believers. One gives the nation while the other gives the doctrine. The fruit of this combination came to be called the national church. In Germany, for example, the Lutheran Church became the national church of that country. The reason for having accepted secular political influence was to provide a counteraction to the strong power of Rome. Yet, this led to national reform, not Church reform. For as a consequence, the Church of Rome was replaced by the Church of Germany, that is to say, the Protestant German Church. In England it became the Church of England (or Anglican Church). This meant that all Englishmen would henceforth belong to the Anglican Church, in that they would be baptized into that Church when they were born. The question then asked is not whether the person is born again but whether one has English nationality. The resulting implication was, therefore, that as long as one is born in England or has English nationality, he is a member of the Anglican Church.

For this reason, the tradition of infant baptism continued to prevail.

Birth of Independent Churches

The rise of these Protestant national churches aroused the dissatisfaction of many who loved the Lord with a pure heart. They were not willing to remain in these national churches. As a consequence independent churches came into being. Not long after the Reformation, in fact, there came to exist more than two thousand independent churches. In Switzerland alone there were more than two hundred of them. During this period, the Roman Catholic Church persecuted the Protestant Church, and the Protestant Church persecuted these small independent churches. For instance, in order to check the growth of these small churches in Britain, the British government passed an ordinance calling for the unification of all churches in the country. And the result? The Nonconformists appeared. These were the people who loved the Lord intensely and who were raised up by God as His faithful ones. They refused to cooperate with Governmental control. So the Government put pressure on them, forbidding their ministers to return to within five miles of their former church parishes. Noncomformists were also barred from taking part in government service. All such who were bona fide civil servants were now relieved of their positions. Whoever violated any of these restrictions would be condemned.

Recovery of the Truths of Believers' Equality and Baptism

In time the Mennonites appeared. They were the first who saw the error of Sacerdotalism [the belief held by the Roman Catholic and other sacerdotal-minded Churches which assumes that an authorized priesthood is required as mediator between man and God, between man and his divine needs and aspirations—*Translator*]. They therefore restored the calling or addressing of each other simply as brothers. Some of them even went to Russia to preach the gospel. Beyond these believers, the Baptists were also raised up. They recognized the error of infant baptism. In Baptist congregations people were now immersed, and done so only after they were clear on the truth of salvation and regeneration. Accordingly, many were nicknamed the Anabaptists [meaning rebaptizers; i.e., rebaptizers of adults formerly baptized as infants—*Translator*] and they were severely persecuted. Nevertheless, the above-mentioned events and groups had mostly to do with the external recovery.

The Recovery of Inner Life

Yet apart from these areas of external recovery, there was also a recovery of the inner spiritual life. Numbered among those involved in this spiritual recovery were Madame Guyon, Father (later Archbishop) Fénelon, and others. These people were commonly labeled as mystics. They learned to deny themselves. They joined themselves to God against

their very own selves. They would not excuse themselves, nor would they plead to be spared. And in
each age since, there have been those who have followed in their footsteps. But God also raised up
other people of the inner life called the Pietists and
the Quietists.

Following these saints, the Puritans, too, were
raised up. Numbered among them were some
brethren from Holland and England who migrated to
the North American continent. The "Mayflower" was
the now famous ship which carried these emigrating
Puritans to America.

The Brethren Recovery

In the preceding century to our own, God engi-
neered a special recovery. This came through the
Brethren movement. God began to raise up believers
who saw the heavenly calling of the Church. Unlike
the children of Israel in the Old Testament period,
the Church—these Brethren believers began to see—
should not expect *earthly* blessing since she has a
heavenly calling. Their goal, they realized, did not lay
in reforming society, for the people of God are nothing more than pilgrims on the earth. They are those
who entertain no hope for the world, since the world
will soon pass away and all on earth will be judged.
The Church, they believed, should hold different
views from those of the world: what the Church expects is heaven, not the advancement of this world.

These words, of course, are quite familiar to our
ears today. But near the begining of the nineteenth

century, they represented a tremendous recovery; indeed, in their day they constituted a radical departure in Church thinking and approach.

The next thing recovered was the unity of the Church. Due to their seeing the oneness of the body of Christ, these Brethren viewed the Church of their day as having fallen into ruin. Bible expositors among them such as J. N. Darby and F. W. Grant believed the present Church to be in ruin.

Recovery of Sanctification by Faith

Apart from the recoveries among the Brethren movement, John Wesley was also raised up by God. Through him the doctrine of sanctification was recovered. Man is not only *justified* by faith, he is also *sanctified* by faith. Wesley was a true servant of God and was greatly used by the Lord. He is our brother, and his witness is true. Though he used the wrong Scripture to prove his point, his doctrine is nonetheless correct. For example, Wesley quoted 1 John 1.7 as proof for sanctification. Some people have rejected his doctrine because of his inaccurate citation. This is over-reacting. For Scripture may be misquoted, but if the man is right and his doctrine is right, his mistake is not decisive. On the other hand, if a person's quotation is correct but his character is questionable, the problem is more serious. Rather is it better to be the right person with the wrong quotation than to have the right quotation but be the wrong person. Even though his Scripture may be misguided, the person can nonetheless be sanctified by God.

After Wesley came Robert Pearsall Smith, husband of Mrs. Hannah Smith who wrote *The Christian's Secret of a Happy Life*. He was a porcelain merchant. At that time people were not very clear on the teaching of holiness. God raised up brother Smith to preach especially on consecration. Sanctification is not just by faith, preached Smith; it also needs consecration: man needs to be sanctified by consecration as well as by faith.

Then there arose the Keswick movement. Among those involved were Evan Hopkins of England, Theodore Monod of France and the aforementioned Smith of the United States. Andrew Murray was also being raised up. These brothers stabilized the work of recovery. At the same time the hymns of Frances Ridley Havergal enriched the recovery.

Recovery of the Crucifixion of the Old Man

Hence in the past century, through all these brethren God caused people to see consecration and its importance. Nevertheless, what they saw still did not go deep enough. This was because consecration is more than a kind of exchange—more than an offering up of all we have in exchange for what God has and is. For example, Darby noted that consecration is based on the putting off of the fleshly man: the aim of the gospel is more than the forgiving of the sins of the sinner: it is also the crucifying of the sinner himself: that is to say, the gospel is also for the *co*-crucifixion of the sinner. How careful must we be in preaching the gospel lest we preach wrongly. The gospel gets rid of the "old man" in the flesh as well as the sins of the flesh. He who is going to heaven is a new man, not an old carnal man. All spiritual lessons—such as obedience, service and so forth—must be practiced in accordance with this principle. Even the lessons learned by such a spiritual person as Madame Guyon must be sought for according to the principle propounded by brother Darby.

Romans 7 mentions that we were made dead to the law (v.4). Hence, we can be married to Christ. We are not just dead to our sins, we are even more so dead to ourselves. It is illegal for anyone who is not dead to self to be married to Christ. Else this would make that person an adulteress. Being dead to self, one is no longer the same person, since the cross has put that person away (Gal. 2.20). Today, whoever is dead to sin is a dead old man (Rom. 6.6). The cross has put away the old man. Such, then, is the gist of Darby's preaching.

Mrs. Jessie Penn-Lewis was then raised up to proclaim the truth of the cross. She told people how to deal with the old man. Her understanding was more advanced. Yet our understanding of today even surpasses hers.

Recovery of the Truth of Resurrection

Following Mrs. Penn-Lewis, brother T. Austin-Sparks saw resurrection in a clearer light. We ourselves have preached resurrection for a number of years, yet I am afraid we were not sure just what resurrection really is. Mrs. Penn-Lewis herself wrote two books on resurrection, but neither was clear on the matter. Not till 1926, when brother Sparks wrote on the subject in "The Overcomer" magazine did the world for the first time see what resurrection truly is. When Miss Margaret E. Barber and I saw the writings of brother Sparks, we were immediately captivated by their message. Many—including ourselves—have talked and preached about resurrection in the past, but the reality of resurrection was not truly known. But when brother Sparks spoke and wrote on resurrection, clear light was finally released.

What, then, is resurrection? Resurrection is life entering into death and coming out of death. In other words, what can die dies; what cannot die comes forth. It is that which death cannot swallow. And such is resurrection life.

Recovery of Kingdom Reality (Welsh Revival)

Let us look at another matter, that of the kingdom. Kingdom is too general a subject. It is therefore futile to talk about the kingdom without having its manifestation. When and where have we ever really seen the kingdom? One instance comes to mind. We may say that the kingdom appeared during the great Welsh Revival. In 1901-2 a great stirring of God broke out in Wales through the instrumentality of Evan Roberts. That revival surpasses all in the past history of the Church. None else can be compared to it. Its effect was deep and wide. At the time of its outbreak Evan Roberts had been a coal miner. He was not a highly educated person, but he was greatly used by God. He was only in his twenties, quite a young man for such a task. He did not know how to preach. Even so, his spirit was strong, and his prayers were heard by God. English was taught brother Roberts by Mrs. Jessie Penn-Lewis as well as by J.C. Williams. Though his education was limited, people got saved as they came into contact with him. He was not at all eloquent and during the Welsh Revival he did not preach much. Indeed, whenever he stood up to speak he usually did so for only fifteen minutes. Yet even those who listened surreptitiously got saved.

Some have said that the Welsh Revival was actually influenced by China. As was said earlier, the Welsh Revival occured in 1901-2; but just a year before, in 1900 during the Boxer Uprising in China, many Christians were martyred.* Immediately after this violent Uprising had been quelled, Christians throughout the world prayed for the work of God.

---

*The Boxer Uprising, known also as the Boxer Rebellion, was a movement by members of a secret society in China whose literal name was "Righteous Harmonious Fist" but whose members came to be called "the Boxers" by Westerners. The society initially was anti-Manchu in character because of reactionary measures taken by the Imperial family and especially by its court followers against carrying out domestic reforms agreed upon following China's humilating defeat by Japan in 1895. But after 1899 the Boxers' chief animosity turned towards those other foreign nations—nearly all European—who had been stripping China of land and power. In June 1900, therefore, the Boxers began a violent campaign to eliminate all "foreign devils" from Chinese soil and to compel indigenous converts (the "secondary devils") to renounce Christianity—the foreign religion of these Western "devils." Though the Uprising ultimately failed of its goals, many Europeans and indigenous Christians in China

And it would appear that the answer to these prayers was poured out by God upon one person in particular: Evan Roberts.* He was subsequently confined to his home from 1903 to 1909 because of illness. After his recovery, however, whenever he stood up to speak he spoke on the kingdom. It was recorded in "The Overcomer" magazine that many times during

---

were killed, and the legations at Peking were besieged by the Boxers for many weeks. An eight-nation Western army, the International Relief Force, pushed its way to Peking from the coast in August of 1900 and released the legation prisoners.

But before the Uprising was finally brought to an end, 250 missionaries and over 32,000 indigenous Christians had been slaughtered! "Westerners were hacked to death, children were beheaded in front of their parents' eyes and carts were driven backward and forward over the half-naked bodies of young Chinese women evangelists until they were dead." So writes the China-born Christian author, Os Guinness of England, whose grandfather, a missionary doctor in China, was an eyewitness to much of the Uprising and who for thirty days had himself "survived the massacre hair-raisingly by the grace of God . . ." Yet, adds Guinness, the retaliation by the Western nations proved to be even worse than the bloody violence perpetrated by the Boxers. "After entering Peking and rescuing the legations," he notes, "some of the foreign troops set off on an orgy of systematic slaughter and looting. Peking was sacked, the imperial palace looted and stripped, and thousands of innocent Chinese were massacred in a cruel and bloody rampage." Guinness, *The American Hour; a Time of Reckoning and the Once and Future Role of Faith* (New York and Toronto: The Free Press, 1993), 7. In the end China was compelled to apologize for the murder of foreign officials and to pay a large indemnity. Interestingly, however, America returned most of its indemnity, inspiring the Chinese government to set aside this sum for financing the sending of students to American universities.—*Translator*

*For a brief discussion of the direct impact in China itself of this worldwide prayer while the Boxer Uprising was actually taking place, please see below, Part Three, Chapter 1 ("The Recovery of Body Life"), in the Appended (c) section therein.—*Translator*

the meetings he was asked what he was going to release in spoken ministry. Yet he himself did not know
what word should be released. But always as he
opened his mouth, something real came forth.

During these years, I began to see what the kingdom of God really is. It is a tremendous matter. I
pray for the kingdom of God because God wishes to
have His kingdom come on earth (Matt. 6.10,33). Yet
for God's kingdom to come to earth, it requires the
prayer of the Church. What, then, is the kingdom?
Kingdom reality is when and where people occupy
geographic territory for God. Wherever the kingdom
of God is, there is God's occupation of that land.
Today people misunderstand the kingdom to be a
historical affair, but it really is a geographic matter.

Recovery of Spiritual Warfare

Yet in order to have the kingdom—that is to say,
to occupy territory for God—there must needs be
warfare. For this reason, the restoration of the kingdom necessitates that there be a recovery of spiritual
warfare. The message on this subject was recovered
by none other than Mrs. Penn-Lewis. While sick on
one occasion, she experienced spiritual warfare. She
came to realize that many were deceived because
they did not understand this kind of warfare. Later,
she co-authored with Evan Roberts himself the book
entitled *War on the Saints,* in which the truth of spiritual warfare was released. Such light had not been
seen for almost two thousand years. This light, of
course, had originally been given by the apostle Paul

in Ephesians 6, but believers since then had failed to experience it. Now, though, it had been recovered through Mrs. Penn-Lewis.

Recovery of the Reality of the Body of Christ

Around 1930 brother Sparks began to see the Biblical concept of the body. Subsequently he often spoke on the body of Christ. His release of such a message amounted to some 500 to 600 pages. Nevertheless, what he released was but words. The reality was yet to appear.

The Church of the Lord is a body. It is the product of our life in the Lord. That life is the Lord's life which is also the life of the Son of God. Since the body comes from one life, the members ought to be coordinated. We cannot be independent. We are parts of the whole. It is like auto parts which, coming from various places, are assembled into a whole automobile. Today we need to see that the life we have in Christ is a *body* life. What we each possess is but a part of that one life. Therefore, we should not seek after personal edification before or ahead of body coordination. Individual building up actually grows out of the coordination of the body of Christ. If we ourselves see this fact, then all who are saved afterwards will themselves immediately see and enter into this fact. As soon as they are saved, they instantly commit themselves to the Church.

Today the gospel lacks authority because there is not the manifestation of the normal Church. In a *normal* local church, as soon as a person gets saved he is a committed one, for he has seen the body. Today too many people, after being saved, have not thoroughly consecrated their lives. Hence we need to return to the lessons of consecration. Due to the lack of a normal Church, we are unable to show the newly saved what is the normal condition of a local expression of the body of Christ. The obstacle stands in our way because we fail to give the remedial lesson. If today there are enough brothers and sisters standing on the ground of God's complete redemption—namely, that upon being saved, believers are immediately wholly consecrated and fully committed—then the local expression of the Church will have the authority to witness for the Lord and bring people to the right standing from the first day of their salvation.

Today's Responsibility of Recovery Is upon Us

The responsibility of recovery is today upon us. The issue of recovery is also upon us. How much God will do in China, nay, in the world, rests upon our shoulders. The responsibility is ours. We need to see that there is but one life in the body of Christ. And after seeing this, we shall also see the need of coordination. Indeed, the problem of brothers and sisters falls upon us. If each of us is not the right kind of person, how can we preach the right kind of gospel? The gospel does not merely cause people to be delivered from sin, the world and self; it even enables us to be liberated from individualism, wealth and everything else so that we may enter into the reality of the body.

The Lord's recovery proceeds step by step. It has advanced so much that today there seems to be nothing more to be recovered. In fact, the extent of recovery has in our day already reached to the recovery of the body. This may be the last stage of recovery, though no one can say for certain. But so far as we know, the coordination of the body and the manifestation of authority seem to be the last areas of recovery.

Yet for us to reach this particular recovery ourselves, God demands that its authority be made manifest in us. For this to be achieved, however, we need to walk in the way of obedience. If we obey, God will be able to obtain the increase among us. Accordingly, today's urgent need is for this recovery to be found in us first. We should be well-balanced persons, that is to say, those who have all kinds of experiences in our lives. The gospel we preach is an all-inclusive one. As people accept the gospel, they are not only having their sins forgiven, they are also being brought into the body of Christ. If we can succeed in this after a few years, the condition of the Church will be totally different from that of today. Today's responsibility is therefore wholly upon us workers.

What we need in our day is body consciousness, for the reality of body life can only be achieved through such consciousness. This, however, is something which can neither be learned nor pretended. In Kuling one brother inquired of me concerning his personal future. His very question, however, closes off the book on his future; for in the body, we do not have personal futures. There is only the future of the body. We would obey the body rather than violate it by seeking to further our personal futures.

Guidance of the Body

As a matter of fact, we make many mistakes in our lifetime. Who is responsible for these mistakes? Of course, we ourselves are responsible. Since we individually tend to err, why not rather be willing to err in the corporate body? Any mistake made in the body will be better than the mistake we may make in ourselves. Suppose today there are three or five, even thirty or fifty, people who know the will of God whereas I myself am uncertain of His will about a certain person or thing. Would it not be better for me to accept their judgment than my own? When anything happens to me, I am subjectively involved. I may not be able to see matters clearly because I am affected by the various factors surrounding that matter. But the body is immune to personal affects. Its judgment, therefore, is more dependable inasmuch as it is being less affected.

Were we not possessed of spiritual reality, such a word might sound like the teaching of the Roman Catholic Church. Indeed, without spiritual reality, portents of the Roman Church will inevitably arise. However, if there be spiritual reality, we will see that the spiritual sense of the body as exhibited in its spiritual members far exceeds our personal judgment. Body consciousness is something which cannot be forced. If a member feels uncomfortable or uncertain, it is wise to submit himself to the body.

Today we must learn to obey God's authority. We see man's rebellion everywhere. In whatever organization, there is rebellion and insubordination. People desire to be free and independent. All have their own opinions and subjective views. But in the kingdom of God none of these things exists. There we find only order and submission. Nothing in the world is better than obedience; nothing is more beautiful than order. There is obedience as well as submission to one another. There is no strife nor seeking to be the greater. A divine order prevails. All seek to submit. How very beautiful is this!

Let me give a little testimony of my own. In 1922 I began to learn this lesson of which we have been speaking. At that time I was often bathed in tears as I learned to obey. Although the person I submitted to might not necessarily have been right and I might perhaps have been right, I had to obey, else I would not receive the discipline of the body. Perhaps I should not talk of this period in terms of the discipline of the body since such language was foreign to me then; but at least I could receive the discipline of the Holy Spirit. This was the time when I started to serve the Lord. I was rather young in age. I had a fellow worker who was five years older than I. He was quite zealous, yet he did not see much. I, through the mercy of God, was given much light. During that period many would admonish people to believe in Jesus, but they could not explain why they should believe. I, though, seemed to have more light on the gospel.

Now on one occasion, more than sixty people had wanted to be baptized. Ninety percent of these were brought to the Lord by me. Since they came to the Lord through me, I naturally felt I should be the one to baptize them. But the other brother insisted that he would do the baptism because he was older. Yet the Bible seems to indicate that he who preaches the gospel performs the baptism (see Acts 8.35-38). I felt that was most reasonable. I later went to see Miss Margaret Barber. She reckoned, however, that I should let that brother undertake the baptism. I asked her why. She said it was because that other brother was older. But then I found another brother who was older than the brother in question. I suggested to her to let this third brother do the baptism. Miss Barber still maintained that the former brother should perform the baptism. Upon hearing this I grew very angry. She told me that I should not argue. She further said, "Look, from today onward, you must learn to listen to his word." Why must I listen to him, I persisted, since he was clear on neither truth nor way? Such a situation continued for three years. But this was the lesson God wanted me to learn. And through such learning I am able to walk together with others today.

The Scriptures record the word of the centurion: "I also am a man under authority, having under myself soldiers" (Matt 8.9). This is submission. I have always felt that an insubordinate person is wild and confused. He who lives in the church should be one who obeys authority. Anyone who is insubordinate, though he may be saved, does not walk like a regenerated person. Whenever a person denies authority, he denies the church. He has no proper way.

God has His anointing oil. That oil is poured upon the Church, the body of Christ (cf. Ps. 133). Therefore, we each need to submit to the anointing oil in the local church as well as to the anointing oil that is upon us individually.

Due to the protection afforded by the body, we as Christians are today most secure. In the past, people might err a long way because there was no demarcation then. But today many truths have been established. We therefore have no reason to deflect from the right way. As we remain in the body, we shall receive the anointing oil and its attendant blessing (Ps. 133.3).

It is imperative for us to see that today's problem rests upon us workers. We should realize the greatness of our responsibility. Owing to our own unfaithfulness, we dare not preach the full gospel to sinners. To preach the gospel that transforms people, we ourselves must be transformed persons. To proclaim a unique gospel, we need to be unique. It takes a recovered person to preach the gospel of recovery. It requires a coordinated man to proclaim the gospel of coordination. Without our being the right person, how can we announce the right gospel? We need to be the people of Acts 2 in order to preach the gospel of Acts 2 and to produce the converts of Acts 2. What can I say to you if you make your family, profession, wealth, or position your center? This only can I tell you: you are unable to be coordinated and the glorious scene of Acts 2 will have no opportunity to appear. How can we expect others to be right if we ourselves are not right? If we are unwilling to be absolute, God will raise up absolute people later on. Whether God finds His way in *this* generation or not depends on whether there are absolute people in it.

Impact of the Gospel

In the early Church, though the saved were relatively few compared to today's gospel harvest, yet they were as a blazing fire. Compared to today, they did not preach as much; but their martyrdom spoke much more than what we do in our entire lives. Today's need is none other than absolute consecration and absolute submission. This will bring in power. In his *Decline and Fall of the Roman Empire*, the English historian Edward Gibbons has described the sufferings of the martyrs: how they were persecuted, exiled and killed by the Roman soldiers. Yet the more the persecution, the greater the number who became saved. Today's issue is, What is the place of the gospel in our lives? The greater its place is in our lives, the greater shall be the power of the gospel.

Whether or not the next generation will be like the people mentioned in Acts 2 hinges on the performance of this our generation. Are we willing to be fully surrendered? Recovery may come to us or it may pass us by. If God finds His way in us, hereafter the saved will be different from those we see today: a better race of spiritual men and women will be raised up. Insignificant are the words and judgments of men; what is important is, What kind of people are we before God?

Our God is an ongoing God: "My Father worketh

even until now," the Son once said, "and I work" (John 5.17). When we lay down our all—including our time and wealth—at His feet, power shall break forth. Can today's call be less demanding than it was in the early days when our Lord called His disciples to lay down their lives for His way? Whereas in the past we persuaded people to believe in the Lord by patting their shoulders and speaking to them a few soothing words, now we call for their lives. Formerly, in believing, people thought they were doing the Lord a favor. Such is not to be so in our day, for they shall see that in believing they must surrender their very lives.

The Way before Us

In order to comply with the work of God, there need to be adjustments made in our future way. Here let me mention a few:

1. The need for training. In training, special attention should be paid to the vessel itself. The vessel must be right before the work to be done by that vessel can be right.

2. The need to strengthen today's work.

3. The need to learn how to discuss and deal with people. Those workers who have been too harsh towards the believers must be restrained, and those who have been too lenient need to be strengthened. In the future, the Bible tells us, we shall judge the world and the angels (1 Cor. 6.2-3). Hence today we should learn how to judge. However, the first to be

judged is our very own self. Unless we judge our *selves*, our judgment of others is faulty. With self-judgment, though, our judgment elsewhere can be accurate. In this respect, the ministers of God's word must truly master this lesson.

4. The need to see that money must have no grip upon the lives of fellow workers. Fellow workers must be delivered from the control of money. Money consciousness should be totally broken. We expect that this will lead eventually to the reality of this: "all that believed were together, and had all things common" (Acts 2.44).

5. The need for the local church to pay attention in learning how to help the newly saved. There should be good preparation for the giving of clear instruction. Such instruction comes in two areas. In one area is the preaching of the gospel. The gospel should be preached throughout the year. The other area is the instruction of new believers. Fifty-two basic lessons should be prepared as a basis for giving continuous instruction to new believers. These should be fixed lessons to be used from the year's beginning to year's end.* Those who instruct should be well prepared with adequate tools.

---

*These 52 Lessons for new believers the author himself soon afterwards prepared and then presented in a sequence of spoken ministry before those assembled for the First Workers Training Session that was convened for several months during the summer and early fall of 1948 at Mount Kuling, near Foochow, China. Of these 52 Lessons, 48 of them were translated into English, re-arranged and variously grouped together into six volumes, and published under the general title of the *Basic Lesson Series* (New York: Christian Fellowship Publishers,

Concerning this matter of consecration, every saved individual should be a consecrated person. All consecrated brothers and sisters work together with the workers.

The Lord told us that "ye have the poor always with you" (Matt 26.11). It is not right to accumulate things in the house of God. To help the poor is a basic principle in the Bible and is demanded of the believer to do. Whether the one in need is of your household or not, the call of God's word is for you to give away. Your heart will not expand if you do not care for the poor. But when you give, you learn enlargement of heart as well as expansion of horizon. Few there be today who have enlarged hearts and extended horizon. We are taught by the Scriptures not to be bound up by material things. And all which the Scriptures teach must be kept. We will suffer loss if we fail to keep any of the Bible's commandments. It is easier to give to the brethren than to the outsiders. Nonetheless, the Bible instructs us to look after the poor—no matter who they be.

Many brothers and sisters are ignorant of the dif-

1972-75). The six individual volume titles in this series are as follows: *A Living Sacrifice* (1972), *The Good Confession* (1973), *Assembling Together* (1973), *Not I But Christ* (1974), *Do All to the Glory of God* (1974), and *Love One Another* (1975). Of the remaining four Lessons, one of them was translated into English and incorporated into the chapter entitled "Sickness" found in Watchman Nee, *The Spiritual Man*, 3 vols. (New York: Christian Fellowship Publishers, 1968), III:179-95. The other three Lessons, also translated into English, appear as Part Two ("Three Basic Lessons") in Watchman Nee, *The Spirit of Judgment* (New York: Christian Fellowship Publishers, 1984), 55-94.—*Translator*

ficult way the fellow workers spend their days. Some workers have not been able to cook any food for five days. Some are not able to take care of their own families' livelihood or their own children's education.

Brothers and sisters should be helped in the choosing of a profession. In body coordination, some need to bring in money. But who will go out and earn money *for the Lord*? Only those who are fully consecrated will do so. Such earning of money is most useful. When the children of Israel left Egypt they brought out the wealth of that land with them (Ex. 12.35-36). Then when they crossed the Red Sea, wealth, too, crossed over. Such wealth would have been unprofitable had it remained in Egypt. Only the people who crossed the Red Sea were able to use the gold and silver to build the tabernacle. So here we see that first of all, men came out; second, wealth must follow out; and third, the tabernacle would be built.

Formerly I dared not say this, but lately I can say that unless people first consecrate themselves, God will not ask for their money. Unfortunately many must see the mistake of the golden calf before they can see the issue of gold. In worshiping the calf idol, the gold which should have gone towards the construction of the tabernacle went instead into the making of the golden calf. Hence, worshiping the golden calf was more than a matter of sin, it also involved a loss to the tabernacle. It was wrong for the gold to go towards the making of the golden calf, but it would have been right for this same gold to have gone towards the making of the tabernacle. Thus we see that the same material could go to either of two diametrically opposite centers: to the idol or to the tabernacle. It is significant that the New Testament places together both covetousness and idolatry, thus showing that they join hands (Col. 3.5). Accordingly, where the deliverance from idolatry is, there also is the deliverance from money and wealth. Today all fellow workers must go forth, bearing all tribulations for the sake of the Lord. But brothers and sisters must also learn to be consecrated people. Saying this does not mean that all should step out to be preachers. It simply means that everyone must be a consecrated person. To be fully consecrated is the need of this day. Not all are preachers, yet all must serve God full time.

Wherever there is a company of people walking in the way of God, there we shall see the appearing of the men of Acts 2. With consecration God finds His way; otherwise, the word of God will suffer and be degraded. The people in Acts 2 are like people arriving at an intersection. They see the way ahead and know how to walk in it; and so they have the boldness to tell others of God's way. The more we harbor fear of people's unbelieving, the more we shall *beg* them to believe. But if we have sufficient spiritual weight, knowing clearly the way to go, we will have courage to speak and people will also dare to believe the *full* gospel. The reason they dare not believe us today is because we ourselves lack faith. But if we workers are clear, others will follow. Yet should we not be clear, we will tend to lower the word of God. Therefore, today's problem lies wholly with us.

2 | **The Ruin and Progress of the Church***

Let us pause for a moment and ask this question: Does the Church today serve the Lord on a ground different from that of the past? Or is the ground of today's service the same as yesterday's? Here we shall discover two aspects that are absolutely opposite and contradictory to each other. Many do not realize that the Church on the one hand is in ruin and on the other hand is progressing.

The View of the Church in Ruin

From one viewpoint, the way the Church has walked during these two thousand years of her history has made her poorer and poorer spiritually. Indeed, from God's viewpoint the Church is in total ruin. Just look at the condition of the Church today: many sins and errors remain in her. Yet not just

*Delivered at Church Meeting on Hardoon Road, Shanghai, 19 April 1948. —*Translator*

today is this true; from the Bible we learn that even the Church in the early days had fallen into ruin. Paul in his day was already talking about the presence of false shepherds, false prophets and false apostles. Though the situation in Ephesus seemed to be, in positive terms, well advanced, nevertheless, it was also declining (see Rev. 2.1ff.). In his Letter to the Philippians, Paul wrote this: "they all seek their own, not the things of Jesus Christ" (2.21). The letters of 1 and 2 Timothy were written not long before Paul's death. There we can also discern the ruinous condition of the Church. For though in 1 Timothy he mentioned elders and deacons (3.2,8), by the time of 2 Timothy he could now only commit the testimony to faithful men (2.2)—as though to say that even the elders and deacons were no longer dependable. Again, in 1 Timothy, Paul had exhorted the elders to be faithful; but by the time he wrote 2 Timothy he could not but acknowledge when speaking of the Church of God that "in a great house there are not only vessels of gold and of silver, but also of wood and of earth" (2.20). Yet not only Paul, but Peter too told us that there would soon be people "denying even the Master that bought them" (2 Peter 2.1). It can be seen, therefore, that the Church neither fell just in the Middle Ages nor began to be taken into Babylonian captivity only in the fourth century: nay, even during the *apostolic age* she had already come into ruin. How appropriate, therefore, for Peter to assert that the time had come for "judgment to begin at the house of God" (1 Peter 4.17).

But there is further Scriptural evidence of the

Church's ruin during the apostolic age. The letters of John were written thirty-odd years after those of Paul. From them we learn that even back then there were people in the Church who did not confess Jesus as the Christ. They were denying that "Jesus Christ is come in the flesh . . . and this is the spirit of the antichrist" (1 John 4.2-3, cf. 2.22). Yet not only this testimony do we have from the apostle John; in his Book of Revelation that was written between 90 and 95 a.d., seven local churches of his day were mentioned by John as having received for the most part disturbing messages from the Risen Lord. Apart from the two churches which received no reprimand, the remaining five churches were all sharply rebuked by the Lord (Rev. 2 and 3). From the fall from first love of the Ephesian church to the spitting out from the Lord's mouth of the Laodicean church, all five of them bespoke the undisputable fact of a fallen condition. The threatened removal of the lampstand from Ephesus and the spitting out of Laodicea were dramatic evidences of major decline and ruin. Though some recoveries did occur, as is learned from Church history, on the whole, ruin was the norm. Indeed, the New Testament Letter of Jude mentioned that there are "certain men [who have] crept in privily, . . . turning the grace of our God into lasciviousness, and denying our only Master and Lord, Jesus Christ" (verse 4).

From the historical standpoint such ruinous conditions continued on. As early as the second century the Catholic Church began to take shape. During the second and third centuries the practices of the local assembly were gradually destroyed. By the early fourth century, at the time of Constantine the Great, the Church had taken upon itself the form of an outward organization.

In the early Church, as soon as people believed in the Lord they forsook the world. All occupations were for the Church, not for accumulating money: "all that believed were together, and had all things common; . . . and they continued steadfastly in the apostles' teaching and fellowship . . ." (Acts 2.44,42). Although the Book of Acts recorded that three thousand and then five thousand were added to the Church, many more probably dared not believe because they were afraid of endangering their positions and popularity. Hence, Pentecost not only draws people in, it also drives people away. Who dares to touch Pentecost? For it demands one's very life.

The conditions of the very early Church are the very opposite of the conditions of the Church today. How can we live on earth pretending that the Church in our day is not in ruin? We should not be like Cain. The teaching of Cain is that in the face of man's fall, one should live as though there was no fall (Gen. 4.3-7). Before Cain there had been Adam. God had commanded Adam to till the ground and added that by the sweat of his brow would he eat bread. This was to be a curse upon Adam for his sin (Gen. 3.19). The error of Cain lay not in his refusal to accept the discipline of cultivating the ground. No, his error lay in his failure to condemn the fall of Adam. For Cain felt quite satisfied as he went out each day to till the ground by his sweat. Here was a person who sinned without having any sinful consciousness. Such is the principle of Cain: that clearly one is in sin and yet he says he has never sinned. On the other hand, as a shepherd Abel watched over the flock. God accepted Abel's offering because he acknowledged the existence of sin and knew the power of the blood. Cain was just the opposite. He acted as though nothing bad had happened and that therefore there was no need of judgment. Today as we live on earth, we cannot but have a sense of ruin. We realize the Church has fallen. How can we be devoid of having any feeling against the fallen condition of the Church?

The View of the Church in Progress

Such is the view of the Church in ruin. Viewing from a different perspective, however, one can say that during these two thousand years of Church history she has always been progressing. Looking at her outward appearance, the Church is indeed in ruin. But inwardly, in the lives of the faithful ones who love the Lord, the recovery of God is growing deeper all the time. Church history is like our personal history. When is life the richest in our personal spiritual history? Is it not this, that when we are saved we are justified, sanctified, and regenerated? that Christ dwells in us, and that the Holy Spirit is our power? All these we receive at the time of salvation. All these riches are in us, though we do not necessarily know that we have them. But when do Christians become poor? The answer is: when they in later days keep losing all their spiritual riches. Days after our salvation, we fall into darkness and trials, and we gradually let go of these riches. Yet in the mercy of the Lord, after some days, we regain that which we had lost. This process repeats itself again and again. In the mercy of the Lord, regaining becomes firmer and stronger than before. And finally, after a certain period, these riches truly become ours. The example of Jacob comes readily to mind. In his lifetime, Jacob fell and rose many times. But before his departure from the world, he could lean on his staff and worship God. All that he had lost had ultimately returned to him. He could return to his God as one saved to the uttermost.

From the Age of Church Fathers to Luther's Reformation

Church history, as was said earlier, is not unlike our personal history. The revelation to be found in the Letter to the Ephesians reaches the peak, though the Church at that time might not have experienced it so deeply. The Church in view in the Letter to the Ephesians is in a condition like to a new Christian. In the progress of the Church, such matters as justification by faith, sanctification, oneness of the Church, gospel preaching, the word of the cross, and so forth become clearer as time goes on. What things are recovered are much more transparent. We can see from the letter to the Corinthian church written by the church father Clement that their understanding of the gospel is not as clear as ours today. Even the truths discerned by Augustine in his *Confessions* and by Thomas à Kempis in his *Imitation of Christ* are not as clearly seen as we today see them. In their various writings there is often sand as well as treasure.

Let us see that the Church today stands in the midst of these two opposite states or conditions. Looking at her outward appearance, the Church is corrupted more and more. But looking inwardly, her quality becomes better all the time. Darby in his writings spoke of the Church as the House of Ruin. Yet many do not realize that there is also the side of the Church which is the House of Revival. Few if any can compare with Paul in revelation. He had such clear understanding of the truth. Unfortunately, he has long since departed the earth. If Paul were still living and you were able to ask him for his opinion about the Church today, he would probably say that on the one hand the visible Church has fallen deeper and deeper, but that on the other hand the inner quality of the Church has advanced better and better.

Truth once recovered cannot be lost again. Take, for example, the truth of justification by faith. Some fourteen hundred years before Martin Luther's time, both the Letter to the Romans and the Letter to the Galatians, which originally dealt with this matter, were already in existence. Yet this truth concerning justification by faith was lost. Imagine it! That within the past two thousand years of Church history, for over a thousand years of it this important truth had been lost to the Church! But it was recovered in the midst of a fiery trial through the instrumentality of Luther in the sixteenth century. Will the Church lose it again—say, after another thousand years? Formerly, people had argued about the truth of justifica-

tion by faith. Now, though, after many had been
burnt and many had shed their blood in defense of
this truth, it cannot be lost again. What the Church
possesses today is now something unshakable. And
all such truths become firmer with time.

From the Reformation to the Present Time

Since Luther's day God has raised up other individuals and groups as instruments for the recovery of
other significant truths. Madame Guyon, for instance, was especially used in the revival of the inner
life. J. N. Darby and the Brethren movement saw the
heavenly vision as well as the crucifying of the flesh.
Pearsall Smith was instrumental in recovering sanctification by faith. George Muller saw faith and put it
into practice as few others have. And Evan Roberts
understood spiritual warfare and prayer ministry in a
remarkable way. Most recently, brother T. Austin-
Sparks has been used to recover both the eternal
purpose of God and resurrection life. We may therefore say that the Church has never been so clear and
so spiritually rich as she is today.

The entire Bible is composed of sixty-six books.
Only one of these has no ending, and that is the
Book of Acts. Why is it that this book has a beginning but no ending? Because today we are still continuing on with the Book of Acts. The gospel has not
been preached to all peoples, and the Lord has yet to
come. Even now we continue to write this book. How
glorious it is for us to read in Ephesians 2 and 4
about the holy habitation of God and the many gifts

with which the saints are to be perfected so that all in the body of Christ might someday arrive at the unity of the faith, and unto the measure of the stature of the fullness of Christ, the Church having built herself up in love! Furthermore, we are told in Ephesians 5 that the Church shall one day be spotless and without wrinkle, holy and without blemish. Today, though, we have not yet arrived at this enviable state. We are thus continuing in the recovery of Christ's Church and the writing of the Book of Acts.

When I was in England some ten years ago, brother Sparks asked me which chapter in the Bible I thought was most difficult to be fulfilled. I said the most difficult aspect to be fulfilled would be the perfecting of the saints as described in Ephesians 4. I explained to him that I was quite worried after reading this chapter of Ephesians. I had confidence in other chapters, but regarding this chapter I wondered how it could possibly be realized. For there seems to have been no way for such a fulfillment even after all these two thousand years of Church history. According to her present condition, this will probably not be fulfilled in the Church till after another two hundred years. In men's eyes it seems that the Lord will never be able to return. Nevertheless, though indeed the visible Church is in a ruinous state, today's issue rests on whether there is a group of people who will stand on God's side and accept His riches, on whether such people are willing to pay any cost to obtain these riches.

On what ground are we standing today? We stand in the midst of these two opposite conditions of the

Church. As to the outside, or external condition, we must learn to condemn such a ruinous state. We need to come out of its fallenness. For this reason, we have to be clear on the ground of the Church. It cannot be an equivocal yea and nay. In the house of God we should separate the vessels of honor from those of dishonor. Vessels of honor are not *born* honorable; they become so through purification. The Bible explains it as follows: "If a man therefore purge himself from these [vessels of dishonor], he shall be a vessel unto honor, sanctified, meet for the master's use, prepared unto every good work" (2 Tim. 2.21). Honor comes from separation. All who do not purge themselves from dishonor remain in dishonor. Who are the vessels of dishonor? All who mix together with vessels of dishonor without any sense of shame. These are of dishonor.

Meanwhile, as to the internal state of the Church, we must also learn to enter into the life of the body, learn to be sons of God, and learn to walk in the way of recovery. What the Lord does today far surpasses that which He has done before. Today's Christians ought to strive to enter into the progressive work of God which He is doing in this age. Only seeing the outward ruinous condition of the Church is inadequate. We must go a step further to see the Lord's present-day work. We have no idea at what point the Lord will stop working. We only know God is currently preparing the temple stones to be fitly framed together. One day all things shall be ready. And that will be the time when the Holy Temple of God is finally built.

Types of the Recovery of the Church

In the Old Testament there are two types concerning the Church. One is the tabernacle, the other is the temple. Many have been the people who have spoken on the tabernacle. Over one hundred books have been written on it. But one can hardly purchase a single volume written on the temple. People pay much attention to the type of the tabernacle, but they neglect what the temple typifies. They consider the tabernacle and the temple to be alike, they being redundant types of each other. The fact of the matter is that these two types are not altogether the same. The tabernacle is temporary and external, whereas the temple is permanent and bespeaks the internal. The tabernacle was built in and for the wilderness, but the temple was built by Solomon in the promised land.

The tabernacle in the wilderness serves as a type of the condition of the Church on earth, while the temple represents before God the permanent condition of the Church in the kingdom. Seeing such light will enable us to understand clearly today's situation. In the Book of Exodus we read that God had first had the tabernacle set up. It then traveled with the children of Israel till it rested in Shiloh (Joshua 18.1). At that time, though, the children of Israel sinned against God: "In those days there was no king in Israel: every man did that which was right in his own eyes" (Judges 21.25). In due course the Philistines became their enemy. Samuel, Saul and David were raised up one after another. But the two sons of old

Eli the priest sinned, and the Israelites were defeated by the Philistines. So the children of Israel thought of bringing the ark to the battlefield. The ark was the ark of the testimony, and it was also the ark of peace. They therefore presumed that the ark could help them. But after the ark had left the tabernacle it was taken captive by the Philistines and placed in the house of their god Dagon. God would not protect Israel because of the ark, nor did He want Israel to protect the ark.

After the ark left the tabernacle, it never returned. It waited to be removed to the holy temple after Solomon had finished building it. Jeremiah 7.12 says, "But go ye now unto my place which was in Shiloh, where I caused my name to dwell at the first, and see what I did to it for the wickedness of my people Israel." Evidently even in Jeremiah's time, people still went to Shiloh. With the departure of the ark from the tabernacle, God too departed from the tabernacle. So that the ark, as it were, had its back towards the tabernacle and its face towards the holy temple. Just such a situation characterizes the condition of the Church today.

At the time of Solomon, the latter went to Gibeon to sacrifice. There on the altar Solomon offered a thousand burnt offerings (1 Kings 3.4). He prayed for wisdom, and the wisdom he received far exceeded that of anybody else. 2 Chronicles 1 tells us that in Gibeon were to be found the brazen altar and the priests. But in the tent of meeting there was no ark (vv.3-5). For the ark had already turned its back towards the tabernacle and had turned its face towards the temple (it was even then in Jerusalem in David's tent). This is the testimony of Jesus Christ, and it is also our way. Our way is in following the ark—yet not towards Gibeon but towards the temple.

Today God is preparing gold, silver, wood, stone, brass and iron for His temple. The building materials for Solomon's temple had all been ready-made, they not having been fashioned at the temple site. Thus they were noiselessly fitted together to form the temple, and then King Solomon appeared. One day the time shall arrive for our own King Solomon, the Lord Jesus, to appear. On that day no sound of working tools shall be heard because all the materials will have been well prepared beforehand (see 1 Kings 6.7). When our Solomon arrives, that will be the sign that the holy temple has been finished. Today there are sounds, but on that day all shall be perfectly fitted together to be the Holy Temple of God.

The Church in ruin is a fact, yet the testimony of the temple has continued on throughout these two thousand years. Truths are being recovered one after another. As a matter of fact the number of truths which have been recovered is quite high. Although all manner of sounds are being heard today, one by one the materials are being gathered. Viewing the matter from the perspective of the building of the temple, the Church of God is unquestionably making progress. All the materials are now being prepared. What is needed is for them to be put together. The work of God today is for the purpose of completing the body of Christ so that all the saints may arrive at the unity of the faith and full maturity in Christ (Eph.

4.12-13). God has been doing this work throughout the ages. But today's work is more advanced than yesterday's. The Lord Jesus once said, "My Father worketh even until now, and I work" (John 5.17). The Lord's work is getting better all the time, and the result of His work is that the Church is becoming increasingly richer spiritually. If we proceed on this way of recovery, we shall not fail to see the working of God in our midst.

PART THREE

THE RECOVERY OF BODY LIFE

1 | The Recovery of Body Life*

We surely know by now that the Church is a body. And if that be true, then our work can no longer be independent but must be related to the body of Christ. People may be very good Christians individually, but as they gather together, their "self" will be exposed. Only those who know body life know how to deal with their own selves, thus enabling them to be rightly coordinated with other people. Someone may appear to have reached the summit of spirituality in an individual way. This, however, cannot be taken as true spirituality. As he walks together with other people, his genuine progress and true dealing with self is revealed. For where self reigns, one can see only himself and nobody else. But if self has been dealt with, then he sees others instead of seeing himself.

---

*This message, together with the four shorter words that are appended at the end, were all delivered at Hardoon Road, Shanghai, 12 April 1948. —*Translator*

Let us always remember that our individual life is but a portion of the whole body of Christ. We must live in the body. In it there is strict discipline. The cross is the way of the body. He who does not know the cross knows not the body of Christ. When relatives live far apart, they can afford to be kind to each other. But in close proximity, they soon can become enemies. When a person lives alone in a house, there are peace and joy. But when two brothers dwell together, they will need to learn the cross. The more people dwell together and the closer they live together, the more necessary will be the cross. Sometimes it may almost seem as though crosses hang all over the person. What man reckons as spiritual progress cannot be counted as such till it is tested in body life. Only that which passes the test of the whole body of Christ is true. No matter how great is the work, how rich the gift, even how beautiful the life, all these are unacceptable at their face value unless they have been placed in the context of the life of the body. As you place yourself among the fellow workers or among the brethren, you begin to realize how sketchy is the cross you know and how little is your deliverance from self.

The first thing to know is the body of Christ. Once people see this, they will spontaneously see the need for coordination. The Lord places His authority in the body. Where is the authority? Where the ministry is, there is the authority. For ministry is authority. We all need to accept our personal limitation. We all must realize that we each have but one ministry before God; hence, we need to work together with other ministries for the full supply of the body. Let us seek for coordination. One member alone is unable to cope with all needs. It requires the coordination of the other members. With coordination, we shall receive the supply of the body in all things. Thus we need to experience the coordination of the members as well as to accept the limitation imposed upon each of us by the life of the body.

Authority represents the Head. In our physical body the eye sees things; yet it is not the eye but the head that sees. Hands and feet are moving; yet it is not they but the head that moves. All the movements of the human body depend on the head. What, then, is ministry in the body of Christ? Ministry is the activity of the Head, who is Christ. When there is controversy with the ministry, there is actually controversy with the Head. It is not that we are at odds with a certain member, we are really at odds with the Head who controls the ministry. In the Bible the preponderance of authority that is mentioned is exercised by delegated authorities. When we say we need to submit to authority, therefore, we mean we need to submit to *delegated* authority. And hence, to obey that authority is to obey the Head. For this reason, God's children must learn to obey.

A ministry has two sides to its manifestation: first, through gift; and second, through authority. Gift is the power of ministry as well as the manifestation of authority (see 1 Cor. 12.4-11). We cannot accept gift without at the same time accepting authority. For example, in our physical body the eye has the ability of seeing. It must be accepted by the other members of the body. Whatever member would reject the seeing eye would deprive itself of the supply of its ability. The same holds true for the body of Christ. If you are a member of Christ's body, you need to accept the gifts of the other members; moreover, you do not need to duplicate these gifts. Today you are not supposed to duplicate the many ministries of other people; all you need to do is to accept their ministries.

Never forget that you are but one member, you are not the entire body of Christ. No one is an all-round person. If a person is all-round, then for all practical purposes he ceases to be a member. For example, auto parts are but parts of the automobile, they are not the entire car. Just so, we as individual members do not constitute the entire body of Christ.

Being members, we individually can enjoy the riches of the whole body. My physical finger, for instance, will never complain of not hearing. My ear will never murmur about not walking. It will not say, "How pitiful that I cannot walk as do the feet!" Just so, there are many diverse gifts in the body of Christ, and all these gifts are for the perfecting of the saints. Because of this, there is never any division in the body, nor is there any different goal, aim or cause. Though the hand cannot speak, it is well if the mouth speaks; for as the mouth speaks, it is as if the hand does so too. The life we each have in Christ is a *shared* life, not a *complete* life. Only as we experience the riches of the other members is the body of Christ truly established. And if this be true, can any member of the body be poor or useless?

Many consider what is theirs is theirs and what is

others is not theirs. This kind of individualistic thinking is the worst thing possible in the body of Christ. Individualism must be exterminated from it. The greatest test of the self life lies in the church meeting, among the brothers and sisters. On the one hand, we do indeed see ourselves as individual members. On the other hand, if we have seen the body life we shall avoid individualism and join with many other members to be the body of Christ. It is much easier to deal with strangers since as soon as they come in they know they have come to the wrong address. But it is most difficult to deal with individualism. For the latter often enters the church unawares. In joining with other members, the self life receives its deepest dealing. Rightly living a coordinated life is the evidence of self being dealt with.

Living in the Reality of Body Life

We need to see body life first before we can discuss the issue of whether the church in Antioch may become centralized. First, body life, then the church in Antioch. If there is the reality of the Holy Spirit, there will not be the necessity of centralization. But in the absence of the reality of the Holy Spirit, the passing of proposals, work plans and decisions will not only bring in centralization but even what is akin to the Roman Catholic Church.

The Roman Catholic Church announces that there is but one Church and that their priests and bishops alone can interpret the Scriptures. Moreover, in its view the Roman Church is the only one.

Indeed, the Church *is* one, but the explanation of the Roman Catholics is wrong. How did it fall into such error? We must acknowledge that their emphasis on the unity of the Church is a correct one, but unfortunately in the Roman Catholic Church man's thoughts, maneuvers, organizations, and so forth have prevailed so as to lead it astray. In reaction to the errors of the Roman Church, Martin Luther brought in two things for us. One was justification by faith and the other was an open Bible. True, in the recovery of the Lord, everyone could now read the Bible; yet this does not mean that in the body all believers may teach the Bible. Unfortunately, some who are not given that gift insist on teaching, thus leading to errors. Somebody may piece together two or three verses in the Bible and invent a doctrine. Yet not only the teaching may be wrong; such error may keep people from God's grace. For when the pseudo-teacher is told of his wrong teaching, he may continue to propagate it instead of acknowledging his error. Such persons are unteachable.

In the Church God sets up teachers (Eph 4.11). The teachers are the ones who interpret God's word. Even in the meeting mentioned in 1 Corinthians 14, the prophets occupy a central place. Not everyone can interpret the word of God (vv.26-32). In the meeting, when those who are able to expound the Scriptures rise up to speak, the rest are to discern. This therefore means that the few who expound do not decide on the truth alone. No, a few speak, but all discern. Even if all should fail to discern, what the prophets say is still to be judged by the Spirit of the Lord.

Now Antioch was not a center, it was not the product of human organization. It was born of the Holy Spirit. When a local church is severed from the Spirit it no longer has any spiritual reality. Furthermore, it has the danger of becoming a centralized church. Such a centralized church development can also happen in our own midst. The fundamental issue is how we live. Are we living in spiritual reality? That is the basic question. Will a local church become a centralized one? The answer lies in whether or not that church is spiritual.

As a historical fact Antioch could never become a central headquarters because it never controlled other churches. A local church should not control other churches; the *work*, though, in contradistinction to a local church, has a larger jurisdiction than just being local. The church in Antioch controlled no other church, but the apostles coming out of Antioch had spiritual authority over many churches. When there is a serious problem in a local church that involves the work, it is brought to the workers for resolution. It is stated in the First Letter to Timothy: "Against an elder receive not an accusation, except at the mouth of two or three witnesses" (5.19). Accusation cannot be made on the basis of rumor. It cannot be judged by hearsay. There must be witnesses, and their accusation had to be delivered to Timothy. Timothy was a worker. He was able to deal with the problem of local eldership because he labored in their midst. Antioch was a local church; Jerusalem was also a local church. So far as the local church is concerned, its development into a central church should never happen. But so far as the work is concerned, that is a different story.

The body of Christ is one. What is manifested in many localities is the same life. And this life is the reality of this body. Work comes forth out of this same reality. This is the Lord's standard. In the light of this standard, our work in our midst exhibits weakness. Individual work can never be compared with body work. We shall come up against a wall if we fail to see this. All works which do not proceed from body life will sooner or later reach an impasse. The Lord has led us to walk in this way of the body. We will not survive if we do not so walk. The Lord has pressed us to ask for help, to be delivered from independent work. Accordingly, the starting point of any work is the oneness of the body of Christ.

This that we have been speaking of can be likened to the electric plant that is one, yet the light which issues forth from it shines in various localities. Though the localities of shining are different, they are all supplied by the one plant. Today, works conducted in various places should exist in relation to the fellowship of the body. We should not set up our own fortresses and defenses in these places. Rather, at different places there should be the flow of the one body life. It is wrong to reduce the churches to local competing kingdoms.

In the New Testament there are two groups of workers brought into view. They are the Jerusalem group and the Antioch group (Gal. 2.8-12). Besides these, there are also other workers mentioned—such as those others cited in the Philippian letter who preach Christ (1.15-17). It seems, however, that God devotes little space to them in His word; on the other hand, He emphasizes both the Jerusalem group and the Antioch group. Consequently, what the Bible emphasizes let us also emphasize; and what it slights let us also slight. The two lines of work on which we must be clear are therefore the Pauline line and the Petrine line.

The appearing of centralization is due to a lack of life. When life is lacking, organization is bound to come in. In the body of Christ, organization is a most heavy burden. In the physical realm, when the body is healthy, you do not feel the weight of your body. But when the body is sick, you feel the burden of body weight. The worse the health, the heavier the sense of its body weight. Indeed, in death the body becomes so heavy that it requires other people to bear it up. So when there is life, it is the body. Without life, it becomes a corpse.

Now the same principle applies to the body of Christ. When life is missing, centralization comes in. For the absence of life requires organization to arrange and maintain everything. As long as there is life in the body of Christ, and no matter how large it grows, it will not create any problem. But once the body is devoid of life and becomes a corpse, it is transformed into a heavy burden.

Today we must not reduce the truth of the local church to a method. Were it to become a method, death would set in; and that death is the deadliest. The question is not whether there is to be a centralized church or a local church. The issue before us is whether or not the church shall rest in truth and in life. I fear method just as I fear a centralized church. The local church should never become a method. Once it becomes that, it becomes very, very heavy. This is today's fundamental challenge.

Appended (a)

*Concerning "Hand Over"**

I would like to say something more about the so-called "hand over" term. Let us never ever put this "hand over" into our teaching. For it is not a teaching; it is merely a remedial measure. Because the matter to which the term has reference was not handled well at the beginning, there is therefore a need to remedy it. Let us be clear that as soon as a person is saved, he should be fully consecrated (Rom 6.6,12-14). He should not wait to have his lack of consecration remedied at a later date. Unfortunately many Christians among us have not done well in this area up to this point; moreover, the Church has failed to present this matter of consecration to them at the outset. Indeed, we may say that today's Church has favored believers by letting them continue on without confronting them on this vital point.

---

*"Hand Over"—A term that was adopted as a way of dealing with the special circumstances confronting both the churches and God's workers at that time. What is presented here is no more than the original concept of consecration found in the Bible.—*Translator*

We will not *ask* newcomers to "hand over" themselves. Rather, newcomers must be shown their need to consecrate themselves. Hence this matter of "handing over" is to remedy the consecration that had not been done well at the beginning. Heretofore the standard of salvation had not been high enough, resulting in the fact that what should have been done at the time of salvation was not addressed or not addressed well enough. Logically speaking, once a person is saved, he ought to be fully consecrated and live wholly for the Lord in spreading the gospel. Accordingly, as soon as people come in, they should henceforth be asked to respond to all which the Lord demands of any disciple of His. By so doing, no one would be saved and still hold fast to the world, waiting for some future day to be consecrated.

In the four Gospel accounts, we find that when the multitude thronged the Lord, the latter made His stringent demand. He explained how one must take up his own cross and follow Him (Matt. 10.38, 16.24). Our Lord had not *lowered* His demand; instead, He placed His requirement very high. He called people to come and He told them how. Each follower must forsake the world and get rid of individualism. In fact, these matters should be clearly settled at the time of salvation.

To "hand over" oneself is now an emergency measure. We today use this term "hand over" only temporarily. Then one day when everyone has consecrated himself, this term shall be eliminated. But because of our initial laxity in this area, the situation must now be remedied.

Yet I am fearful that after some days this expression of "hand over" will become a fixed terminology. It is even possible for the application of "hand over" to assume a strange way. Bible teachers, for example, will question what the Scriptural basis for "hand over" might be. There is, of course, no such term as "handing over" in the Bible. Let it be known that we today only talk about "handing over" because Christians in the past have not begun well. If all had started out right, there would be no need for the matter of "hand over" today.

How great is the difference between being well saved and poorly saved. It can be likened to the birth of children: one might weigh only 12 ounces while another might weigh 12 pounds. Ministers of the Church have the responsibility of giving new believers a good start. A good or bad start will result in a great difference as to their future walk. Among those raised up by the Lord in the past centuries, many of them had a good beginning. Because they commenced well, they could proceed well. If the beginning for a saint is clear, the walk shall be straight, regardless the degree of understanding or seeing. But if the beginning be confused, the future is questionable. Therefore, immediately after a person is saved he must be challenged to make a clean break with sins and with the world. The issue of money must also be resolved, and the matter of consecration, including that of individualism, must be settled. Thereafter, what lies ahead for him shall be in God's hand, even as Paul, after bringing people to salvation, committed them to the grace of God (Act 13.43, 20.32).

The future days depend on the grace of God, but at the beginning of a believer's walk, these problems must be clearly addressed. For with a bad start, it will be difficult to remedy the situation later on.*

Appended (b)

The Minister of the Gospel

There are at least six approaches to the preaching of the gospel. The preaching may lay stress on love, righteousness, judgment, sin, the world, or vanity. Yet whatever approach one may use, each needs the working of the Holy Spirit. The result of the Holy Spirit's working is one; which is, that it causes people to capitulate. The true gospel will always convict and convert. Whoever thinks that he does God a favor by believing is being totally foolish. If one really sees the gospel, and regardless whether he meets with love, righteousness, judgment or whatever, he is always "softened up" by the Holy Spirit.

Whenever we preach the gospel we must set before the people the straight path. The issues surrounding the world as well as service must all be resolved. Let us see that the center of the gospel is God, not we ourselves. It is not what we get, but what God gets. As a person receives salvation, he must recognize that henceforth all belongs to God. As

---

*For further helpful amplification of the term "hand over," see a few pages hence at Appended (c). —*Translator*

soon as a person is saved, we should tell him that hereafter he is no longer an independent individual but that he now belongs to the body of Christ as one of its members. Therefore, he must learn to listen and obey.

If the Church fails to walk in this way, it will forever remain below standard. According to truth, the Church is always obedient. But sometimes we ourselves need to return and learn obedience. If we who are God's workmen walk aright we shall work all these matters through with the newly saved. The saved must have a good beginning.

The gospel is not only to be preached but also to be lived by us who preach. It must be seen as well as heard. Preaching is not as powerful as martyrdom. The latter gains more people than the former.

The true story is told of a sister in the Lord who was only about 19 or 20 years old. For the sake of the Lord she was exiled to Siberia to be punished. On the way in the train she comforted her family by telling them, "Do not weep for me, weep for those without God. What I have far exceeds what they have. For in loving my Lord, I gladly suffer for Him. My suffering can never be compared to what my Lord had suffered." At that time there was a thirteen-year-old lad sitting nearby. He was greatly moved upon hearing these words of hers. And as a result he believed in the Lord and later on he became one of those who was greatly used of God in the southern part of the Russian Empire.

Strictly speaking, we workers need to be the kind of men portrayed in Acts 2 before we can preach the word of Acts 2 which they preached. What we must do today is more than preach God's word; we ourselves must have an impact upon the people. And were the gospel to be propagated in such fashion, a fleshly person would dare not come to the church. People with such a life as those in Acts 2 will have an impact upon the assembly and will pass on their zeal and joy. Life is a matter of consciousness, of sensation. You may shake hands with someone and fail to touch any spirit in him. You are unable to touch the real person. But if that person carries with him the things of God, he will cause others to touch those very things. A person with God's life enables others to touch life.

All God's appointed ministries have the Lord's word. A person with ministry usually carries within him some weighty words. These words constitute his burden. Even though sometimes the burden seems light, yet the more it is discharged the more it is increased. It can be likened to a woolen ball whose string you draw out. The more you draw it out, the more woolen thread you will have. All worthwhile ministries are ministries with burden.

Some while speaking speak from their mind. Their mind is actively turning all the time. So that what is spoken are mere words, empty words. As people listen, only the sound enters them, but not the spirit. All true ministries must have burden in the words uttered. A man with true ministry goes forth with a heavy burden inside him, but when he returns home his inside is light, for the burden has been discharged. If a person has no burden, his speaking or preaching is of no use, no matter how actively he uses his brain or how eloquently he speaks with his mouth. A ministry has its ministerial burden. The painful thing is that sometimes when one comes with a burden he may not find an audience that will receive the words. This results in carrying back the burden he had originally come with.

Appended (c)

Know the Supply of the Body

I am convinced that in our present situation we need a drastic deliverance. Men are naturally rebellious and individualistic. They are unwilling to hand themselves over. But today for the Lord's sake we are willing to lay down ourselves. This is the meaning of the term "hand over," a term we have adopted in dealing with our present circumstances. (We hope people would not view it as traditional terminology.) Some may find themselves unable to hand themselves over to the Lord. But if they try, we believe that as soon as the sacrifice is on the altar, the altar will sanctify the sacrifice. It is similar to the situation in which some say they cannot believe because they have too many problems; yet as soon as they believe, all their problems are resolved; they now exercise their faith in Jesus in spite of their doubt and problems. The same shall be true in this matter of handing over: if only a person is willing, God will do the work. Now if anyone has a problem in handing himself over to the Lord, let him ask a few in the local church to help him. And as he makes a positive move, God too will move.

Let us be clear that the "handing over" we are talking about today is not only an individual "handing over," it is a "handing over" through corporate fellowship. It is not as though man attempts to lay himself on the altar and God attempts to accept him. Not so. The fact of the matter is that whether this is a trying or a real handing over, God will always accept. By handing over oneself, one commits himself to the body of Christ. But in turn the body serves as a great protection. In time we shall see what loss we suffer if we do not live in the reality of the body, for the supply of ministry is there. Being separated from the body separates a person from the supply of ministry.

The Book of Acts tells us that when Paul was in Athens "his spirit was provoked within him" (17.16). But when Silas and Timothy arrived in Corinth, he immediately received encouragement (18.5). This that Paul experienced can be likened to the way you sense supply when a certain brother passes by or when a new brother comes to the meeting. Sometimes just having certain brethren sitting there, even without the need of their speaking to you, you receive spiritual supply in ministering the word of God.

Because we are a body—even the body of Christ, therefore we naturally affect one another. We cannot comprehend how this mutual influence works, but we sense a special intimacy with the Lord or experience some unusual sensation. This is because in the body of Christ there is a supply. Indeed, the life of the body is that supply. Let not any brother or sister be a waster of this body supply. Instead, let all of us learn well to recognize the body and our relationship to it. For if there be any failure or wastefulness on our part, such will be largely due to our being *individual* Christians rather than coordinated members of Christ's body.

In 1900 at the time of the Chinese Boxer Uprising, many Christians, as noted earlier, were martyred.* Now it so happened that during the initial stages of the Uprising, the Churches throughout the world had begun sensing that something dramatic and most alarming was about to happen. Many were pressed in their spirit for a number of days and felt the need to pray. One such believer was Miss Margaret Barber who was in England at the time. She has since testified how deeply distressed she had been in her spirit and how she had felt the urge to pray. Such a sensing for the need to pray by so many around the world had not come from the knowledge of seeing and hearing; its origin had arisen instead from the reality of the body of Christ. Very soon thereafter came the brunt of the Boxer Uprising in China and the subsequent martyrdom of literally tens of thousands of God's people there. Who would dare to say that the faithful martyrs of that day did not receive a supply as a result of such a worldwide prayer ministry in the body of Christ?

---

*For a brief informative historical sketch on the Boxer Uprising, please see earlier, Part Two, Chapter 1 ("Commencement and Continuance of Recovery"), in that chapter's subsection entitled "Recovery of Kingdom Reality (Welsh Revival)." —*Translator*

When any part of the body is sick, all other parts of the body rise up together to deal with the sickness and to help this sick member. Just so, in the body of Christ there is a supply that is available to any needy members. The life of the body of Christ is not an empty set of words. It is a reality. Many consider the Church to be nothing but a mystical, abstract entity; they do not realize that this entity we call the body of Christ is a reality. 1 Corinthians 11.29 mentions this very matter of discerning "the body." Here, this phrase has two meanings: (1) the body of the Lord; and (2) the body of Christ—the Church. Here it simply mentions the body, without specifying the Lord's body or the body of Christ. And hence, it points on the one hand to the Lord's own body and on the other hand to the body of Christ which is the Church. This body has the Lord's own riches and it also has the riches of Christ. Every Christian, being in the body of Christ, receives the supply of the Lord's grace as well as the supply of the Holy Spirit (see Phil. 1.19). Nevertheless, the great lack among Christians today is in not knowing the supply of the body of Christ. May the Lord show us the reality of this body that we may know its supply.

Appended (d)

Concerning the Rule of Offering

The Bible mentions several different areas of offering. We would focus on but two of these areas.

First, there is the offering of wealth. The Scriptures do not specify how much wealth one ought to offer. There is no fixed principle. Some offer more, some offer less; and some offer their all. Jesus said to the rich young ruler, "Sell [all] . . . which thou hast, . . . and come, follow me" (Matt. 19.21). John the Baptist declared: "He that hath two coats, let him impart to him that hath none" (Luke 3.11). The Gospels tell us to take care of the poor. The Epistles advise the local church to care for the widows in their midst as well as to look after their own households. This we see in 1 Timothy 5.16,8. And 2 Corinthians 8.15 admonishes us as follows: "He that gathered much had nothing over; and he that gathered little had no lack."

Today's problem does not lie in how much to offer, but in how tight a grip money has on a person. In God's work it is impossible for anyone to retain money on the one hand and to say on the other hand that he loves the Lord in his heart (see Matt. 6.24). For the Lord declares: "where thy treasure is, there will thy heart be also" (v.21). In order not to allow money to control us, we must send it out. As money goes out, the heart also goes out. If a person loves the Lord, he is willing to be poor voluntarily. Voluntary poverty is the way for the release of the heart. Sometimes God asks us to sell everything. Sometimes He calls us to give what is left over. In any case, the heart must be set free. It is recorded in the Book of Acts that the apostle reprimanded Ananias for lying to the Holy Spirit about the fact that he had held back part of the price of his sold land though pretending he had given it all to the Lord (Acts 5.4-

5). Today we should not have anything left over. To have something left over is a shameful thing in the church. All the excesses should be distributed. Yes, we of course need to live. We must look after our own personal necessities and those of our families. But if we are able to set aside just a fraction of our income by lowering our living standard a little, we will have something left over to give away.

In our discussion about "handing over" we were not aiming at the management of money; rather, we had in mind the need of offering to the Lord and for the gospel's sake. The Lord wants brothers and sisters who hold a profession to have ministries through their professions. These years we are in lack of new workers, both men and women, to come forth. Formerly at our peak we had almost four hundred fellow workers. Now we have but two hundred, which means that two hundred are missing. In order to replenish these vacancies in the work we need a group of people to go out and earn money. In the past I dared not mention this; but today I dare to say that some people should go out and earn money and bring that money in to the church for the service of God. In other words, some brethren should offer themselves to earn money for the Lord and for the sake of the gospel. Perhaps one might earn even as much as a million dollars. He would take from that only what would be needed for his own living and give the rest to the church.

Naturally God does not want us to go to an extreme on this issue. He wants us to be balanced. He asks for "us" first and then for "ours" (see 2 Cor.

12.14). We ourselves must first come, and then what is ours will follow. If "we" do not come, God will not want to have "ours." Brothers and sisters must see that all is the Lord's; everything centers upon Him. Though some may fulfill their ministries by earning money and some others may do so by the ministering of God's word, the center must ever be the same: it is the Lord.

Let us note that apart from the offering of wealth, the Bible also mentions a second area of offering; that is, the offering of our occupation or profession. Yet the Scriptures show us that not all professions can be taken up by a Christian. Money surely needs to be earned, but *how* it is to be earned is equally important to consider. There are ways of earning money which are disapproved of by God. We can only take the professions approved by Him. We should not be occupied with jobs of which He disapproves. Today leading brothers in many places do not have the right concept concerning occupations and professions. They have brought this wrong concept into the Church and the Church is therefore adversely influenced. May the Lord have mercy on us.

A Prayer

O Lord of work, we ask You for men for the Church's sake. Today the Church lies in ruin. There is a lack of personnel. May You give men to the Church. May You give all kinds of gifts to the Church. O Lord, have mercy on us. Grant us men and women who are consecrated, handed over to You, and submitted to

Your mighty hand, so that we may serve You with all the saints. We especially ask You to be merciful to us during this time of ruin. Raise up young people, raise up fellow workers. Cause the Church to maintain Your testimony on the earth. May more people place themselves in Your hand that their professions, positions and dwellings be worthy of the gospel. May young people rise up to offer themselves to You for Your work. May brothers and sisters be partakers of the gospel. We believe You can do the work of recovery. May You do a more complete work by raising up more people who will serve You full time and will go out with the gospel. We ask You to raise up a multitude. We do not ask for money and time, but we first ask for their entire beings. Let people consecrate immediately and absolutely. May You take away the ruin and give us people. O Lord, be gracious to us. We ask You for men. The Lord alone is worthy to possess us. You alone can cause us to serve You unconditionally and single-heartedly. We are willing to pour upon the ground the precious water of Bethlehem [see 2 Sam. 23.15-17]. May there be no one who draws back, no one who hides away, and no one who stands by. May the Lord be merciful to us. In the name of the Lord Jesus Christ. Amen.

Absoluteness of Truth and the Relationship between the Body and Its Members*

The Absoluteness of Truth

In doing God's work there is one basic lesson among many that we must learn, which is, to be absolute to the truth. No truth in the Bible is according to man. Today people are not absolute towards truth because they subjectively relate it to themselves. If truth is associated with man, then he cannot speak truth which he has not personally experienced. Yet truth itself is absolute. It is not subject to man's experience. On one occasion David had declared that all men are liars. When he said this he had not thought to except himself. To the contrary, before God he reckoned *himself* to be included in the truth that all men without exception "speak falsehood every one with his neighbor" (Ps. 12.2). God's servants should not look within themselves, for God's truth is pure and it transcends them and us. For this reason, we need to set ourselves aside.

---

*Delivered at Hardoon Road, Shanghai, 17 April 1948. —*Translator*

How often we bend the word of God to suit our situation. Frequently we force God's truth to follow us. We connect truth to ourselves, therefore we insert ourselves into truth.

Last year two brothers came to me and asked whether what the responsible brothers had done in a certain matter was right. My answer to them was that because they were not the responsible brothers they considered it wrong, but that if they themselves had been the responsible brothers they would have reckoned it right. This underscores the fact of how men may affect the truth.

Let us see that what we are has nothing to do with God's truth. If a truth falls under the influence of man, it no longer is truth. Unless truth is absolute in your life, you will neither know how to study God's word nor how to really know God.

We must not judge truth by people's relationship with us. If they are on good terms with us, we say their opinion or assumption is truth; if, though, they are not rightly related to us, we proclaim their assertions as false. As soon as truth is touched by human relationship, it turns into something else. Your way will not be straight if truth is not absolute in your life. Truth should never be swayed by the considerations of men. Not because you are my fellow-student or -countryman, therefore you are right. Many problems in the world and many diverse teachings are attributed to human reasoning. Truth itself never changes.

What is meant by the absoluteness of truth? Paul's First Letter to Timothy mentions the pillar of truth (3.15). Why refer to it as the *pillar* of truth? Because a pillar is something immobile. It can neither be raised nor lowered. It is not like a chair that can be moved about. Unless we are pure in heart, truth will have no affect on us. For truth cannot be entrusted to those who follow their emotion. This is a real test. Men ought to stand on truth's side even if it be against themselves. Only then can they maintain the truth instead of supporting themselves. He whose self has never been dealt with will never know what truth is. For when he is wrong, he will lower the truth; and when he is right, he will raise the truth.

He is like an elevator, with truth being lifted up or lowered according to his every whim. Only those who have dealings with themselves are able to maintain the truth. Thank the Lord, *He* is the elevator, and *He* lifts us up or down.

The main reason for today's darkness lies in our forcing truth to follow us. If you take truth as sole standard and if you dare proclaim that whatever the Lord says is right, then a new light and new way will come to you. Otherwise, you are the only good Christian in the whole world; everyone else must follow you, and even the truth must follow you. He who tries to be convenient to himself is not of much use in the Lord's hand. But if a person can say before the Lord, "this is truth and I am wrong," that person has not bent the light and light will lift him higher. Blessed are they who follow the truth. Hopeful are they who judge themselves. Those who fail to follow the truth but tend to pull it down to their standard shall forever be in darkness and light will never shine upon them.

On the one hand we cannot preach what we have not experienced. Yet on the other hand we need to understand that truth is not subject to us. When we are afflicted and condemned by the truth, we receive light. And such is the basis of revelation, the secret of having revelation.

From ancient to modern times, from East to West, whoever has seen the light does not bend God's word. If I am behind, I must pursue and follow the word of the Lord. I must confess that I have sinned. Then the way will become clearer. The more I walk, the more light I receive. Otherwise, it is all vanity, both in the studying and in the preaching of the truth. Human affection should never affect God's word.

If a thing is right, we must do it. If it is wrong, we must not do it. Let us see that God's word is right and we are wrong. I personally may have some problem with you, but it has no effect upon truth. God's work suffers through human relationships. Truth is not absolute because it is influenced by men. If we sacrifice truth today, what will happen to the next generation? Or to people a hundred years later? They will not be able to see the truth. To be absolute we must pay a very big price. But in so doing, others will be blessed.

I must determine to draw near to the pillar of truth. Indeed, I will not move the pillar two feet; instead, I will move my chair two feet towards the pillar. I can move, but truth's pillar should never be moved. I can change, but the pillar cannot change. How many change truth because of human relationship, history, or sentiment.

Relationship between the Body and Its Members

Today we ask for God's mercy that we may be taught a remedial lesson. We must come to see that what God's children receive is not an individual life but a corporate life. *God* looks upon us as constituting one *body*, whereas *we* notice only individual *members*. For example, here before us is a sheaf of wheat. We may only see grains of wheat, yet in actuality it is one sheaf. Again, a loaf of bread, according to our focus, is made up of many grains of wheat. Our focus is elsewhere than on the loaf. Let us see that in Christ ours is a corporate life. We should therefore not ask when individuals become the body. For the body is not formed by calculating and adding up the members; instead, out of the body comes forth those many members. No, the real question to be asked is, When do we become individuals out of the body? or, When is there individual life in the body? The Bible speaks of the Church as the body of Christ. Accordingly God emphasizes the body, but we tend to emphasize its members.

In speaking of the Church, 1 Corinthians 12.12 makes this observation: "the body is one, and hath many members." Here the body is first being mentioned, and *then* the members. With us, though, the order of our priorities is reversed: we usually commence with the members and then go to the body. But the Biblical order shown here is that the body is mentioned before the members are. In other words, first there is the *corporate* life; and then, after returning home, there is the *personal* life. These two approaches indicate two different grounds. Difference in ground produces difference in consequence. In standing where I presently am, I may see a certain star. But if I should stand two steps farther away, I may no longer see that star. The ground we stand upon is therefore most important. Today we would stand on the ground of the body.

The life we have received is body life. Accordingly, only after we go back home do we take up our personal walk.

Let us realize that our local church life is corporate in nature. Today, however, we tend to see it as primarily personal in nature. Our personal experiences and even our conscience are all personal. But in the future we shall see the conscience of the church. Whenever we have an important decision to make, we should learn to touch the body and to have fellowship with the brethren who are spiritually ahead of us. Let us not assume that it is a difficult matter to seek out advice. In reality, to be asked for advice is maybe something equally as difficult. For no one likes to be put in the position of appearing to meddle in another's affairs. No one has so much interest in other people's lives. Things are complicated and responsibility is great. Nevertheless, if we wish to pursue the corporate way, we must have fellowship. What you eat and wear are matters belonging to the Adamic realm; hence, they are personal in nature. But if you should exceed the personal boundary by spending all your earnings in gluttonous behavior, then you need to be dealt with corporately for it has now become a body matter. Suppose, too, that a sister dresses beyond Christian modesty; then she should be spoken to about it, since this has now become a matter of caring for the Lord's corporate testimony. These interventions cannot therefore be deemed as constituting "busybodiness" on the part of the church.

Some people like to be heads apart from Christ. These are the true busybodies. No authority should be delegated to them. Authority is received from the Head. Before our words have authority in them we need to see the Head, that is, to see that the Lord is backing us. We have no interest or intention to interfere with the affairs of other people. All who love to tamper with others' lives or love to be heads should step aside. Otherwise, those who seek for prominence will become the dictatorial ones. In the body of Christ neither wantonness nor dictatorship is right. The spiritual ones, those who have weight before the Lord, should alone stand up and speak. Not that we *like* to speak, but that we *have* to speak as before God. Actually, those who naturally do not like to meddle in others' affairs or who have no lust to speak should be the ones to rise up and speak; whereas those who are naturally inclined to meddle should be under restraint. What we require is the coordination of the body, not the coordination of the flesh.

In our physical bodies the feet are not as comely as the head. Accordingly, we wear shoes more than we wear hats. In the church, the stronger members of the body are able to supply more, and the weaker ones need to receive more (see 1 Cor. 12.22-24).

3 | The "Body" in 1 Corinthians 12*

1 Corinthians 12 is a very brilliant chapter in the Bible. It reveals the relationship which exists between the Holy Spirit and the body of Christ. Our becoming one body in Christ is dependent upon the Holy Spirit. What joins us together is the Holy Spirit and what we receive inwardly from the Lord is also the Holy Spirit.

Let me use an illustration here. In foreign countries people use cement blocks in the building of their houses. On the outside these blocks look like the bricks in China, but they are hollow on the inside. Now when the construction workers build walls in other lands they fill the blocks with cement and also pave them together on the outside with more cement. The nature of the blocks' exterior and that of their interior are therefore precisely the same. Even so is it with the body of Christ and its members: we—

---

*Delivered at Hardoon Road, Shanghai, 18 April 1948. —*Translator*

as the members of Christ's body—were baptized together into one body by one Spirit and were all made to drink of one Spirit (v.13). What is outside and what is inside are the same. And thus did we become one body with its many members.

Hence, that which unites us is exactly the same as that which we receive from the Lord. Spiritual fellowship is based on the same principle as spiritual life. We can therefore say that the body of Christ is one because it has the same nature as its life. And its life is the life of the Holy Spirit whose nature is one. The oneness of the body comes from the oneness of the Holy Spirit. Let us understand that members come out of the body. Though many are the members, the body is one (v.12). In short, the origin of the members is the body. It is the body which produces many members and it is the Holy Spirit that joins them into one body. It can be likened to a wall that is made up of many bricks, and in turn its many bricks form the one wall. Oneness constitutes more than there being one mind: it signifies the possession of one nature. Having therefore drunk of the Holy Spirit and been baptized in the Holy Spirit—such constitutes the oneness of the saints. We as members come out of the body and, again, we return to the body. Looking backward, a person can see one body; looking forward, he can likewise see one body. And because we as members are one, we can be coordinated.

Due to this oneness, there is body consciousness. The movement of the Holy Spirit is in the body. The Holy Spirit is not just the power of individuals; He is even more so the power of the body that comprises those individuals. Body ministry is the manifestation of the power of the Holy Spirit. Before God an individual is like a two-dimensional plane; the body, however, is like a three-dimensional cube. Today the age of independent work is past. The gospel needs to be preached by the church as a body, but so must matters which come before it be dealt with by the church as a body. In the past, individuals may have worked effectively, but now all needs to be done in and through the body. As we touch the body, the far greater power of the Holy Spirit will be manifested. Many times matters cannot be solved by just one or two brothers. Many of God's people think the power of the Holy Spirit is given merely to individuals: brethren, they believe, can simply bring home as it were a power package of the Holy Spirit and gradually use it. But we ought to know that the power of the Holy Spirit resides in the body.

We believers too frequently consider ourselves as members first and only secondarily do we view ourselves as a body of members that came into being through baptism. The fact of the matter is that we *begin* as the body. Whether or not we like it, we each are members of the body. If we as believers stand on the ground of the individual, we shall lose the powerful corporate effect of the baptism in the Holy Spirit. The body proceeds from oneness and returns to that oneness. How we need to readjust our understanding of truth here. Today if all Christians were to stand on the ground of the body, everything could be resolved easily. But when they do not stand on this ground, they create many problems—problems which emanate from a spirit of individualism. In the body there is the corporate life. Whatever rebels against the body as well as against the Head does not belong to this corporate life.

Let us acknowledge where the riches of the Lord are to be found: they are in the body. For example, with the body comes God's light. As a matter of fact, the body is a "storehouse" of light; therefore light is fullest in the body. Yet so, too, is it with all the other riches. Hence, what one cannot obtain in himself can be secured in the body. As an individual member, each believer has his specific function. But that which one member lacks is found in the body's other members. Indeed, their functions become the possession of the individual members. Thus there is mutual help to be found in the body.

The Love of the Body

Love in a fuller measure can be found in the body of Christ. In referring to it, Ephesians 4 mentions "the building up of itself in love" (v.16). Only in the body can we know what love is in its fullest. We are told in Revelation that the church in Philadelphia had manifested itself in love rather than in doctrine. 1 Corinthians 12 tells us that "whether one member suffereth, all the members suffer with it" (v.26). And Ephesians 5 speaks of the love in the body of Christ, "for no man ever hated his own flesh" (v.29). You may see people beat up on others' bodies but you rarely see them beating up on themselves. In the love of the body there can be the speaking of the truth (see Eph 4.15). But you cannot admonish a person who is outside the body. Only in the love of the body may you so persuade. Outside the body no frank talk in truthful terms is possible, yet in the love of the body such talk can take place. In the body alone is there real love.

Many words in the Bible are hard to put into practice if there is not the proper setting for them. They can easily be obeyed or carried out, though, if there is the body of Christ. For example, the Bible says that we are all priests. But suppose you tell a "lay" member of a denomination that he is a priest. If he should accept this Biblical truth of the universal priesthood of believers, then at the next communion service of his congregation he may wish to go forward to assist the pastor, saying: "You and I are both priests. We both, therefore, can officiate in the communion." Immediately, trouble will arise. For such a word has no way to be implemented in their denominational context or setting. Or take as another example, this: Suppose a person talks about guidance but ignores body life. Confusion will quickly arise, for guidance is in the body just as love is in the body. No correct result will come outside the body context.

Let us see and understand that love and authority are in the body of Christ to deal with the flesh. If we are truly living in the body, nothing will stumble us.

4 | Exercising Authority in the Body and Body Consciousness*

The Tongue and Body Life

In the area of discipline the tongue must first be controlled. For it is the most difficult element to be put under control. One who has a controlled tongue dares only to utter the words of the instructed. Let us realize at the outset that the one who is not disciplined in words is a loosely controlled person.

In London I once met a Christian couple who were insubordinate to their responsible brothers in the assembly. Both husband and wife were nice people; only, they were too talkative. They acknowledged that whenever they spoke in a provoking manner their spirits were irritated. Let us realize that when our words are uttered, our spirits come forth. Both 2 Peter and Jude mention this matter of slander, and slander is done through speech. If we carelessly vilify

---

*Delivered at Hardoon Road, Shanghai, 28 April 1948. —*Translator*

the brothers ahead of us, we easily destroy the unity of the church.

But our listening to slanderous words bears equal responsibility to our uttering slanderous words. To be or not to be a garbage can is one thing; to receive or not to receive garbage is another. One of the reasons for the division and destruction of the Church is the slanderous words of men. For the sake of the unity of their church, brothers and sisters must resist such slanderous words.

Michael occupies the highest place among the angels. In the beginning he was evidently under Lucifer. Although Lucifer has now fallen to be Satan, Michael "durst not bring against him a railing judgment, but said, The Lord rebuke thee" (Jude 9). Michael referred to a higher authority to rebuke Satan. From this we may see the importance of speech.

Some people's tongues are very oily. Such persons do not and cannot know the body of Christ. They will unconsciously destroy the body with their very words. Having a wound is bad enough for a person, but having sand rubbed into the wound as well makes it even worse. Such is the adverse effect of slanderous words. If the tongue is not brought under control, all other controls are false (see James 3.2). Man's tongue is most slippery. The double-tongued will sooner or later discover that he has no one to speak to because he has driven away all his audience. If you are a curious person with an itching ear, you love to have people talk with you to relieve your loneliness. But those who have been instructed of the Lord need to reprimand the curious.

The consciousness of sin comes from the knowledge of God. On the other hand, the consciousness against engaging in or receiving a slanderous word comes from knowing the life of the body. For any slanderous word is opposite to the testimony of the body of Christ.

Learn Not to Be Head

The head expresses its headship through its thoughts and intents. Thus in the body of Christ, for a member to obey the authority of the head is quite simply for him to refrain from entertaining many ideas and opinions. Hence the Christian who lives in the body and observes body life may be said to be a simple person.

There is a basic difference in the understanding of the Bible by the Protestant Church and the Roman Catholic Church. The latter considers the Pope and this Church's hierarchy to be the only ones who can interpret God's word, whereas the laity, this Church believes, should not comment on it. Indeed, the decision of the Pope and his Council is final. Thus, many forms of idolatry have been the result; such, for example, as worshiping the image of Mary. On the other hand, the Protestant Church takes a more liberal stance on the matter than the Catholic Church. For its teaching carries within it the implication that there are as many popes as there are Christians! For its teaching holds that everyone may read the Bible and each may decide on the Bible's interpretation. Yet if we have light, we shall see that both are wrong; because in the body, only certain members whom the Lord sets forth therein have the authority to interpret the word of God. Hence, let us not hasten to be popes.

We may illustrate this matter in the following way. Concerning the paths of life, the Lord has raised up in the local church certain brothers to help us in this matter. If any one of us has a problem with regard to the path of life he should pursue, he can go to these brethren for instruction. Thank God that in the body there is not just one brother who can supply you with life; there are several others. Yet if you desire their ministry, you will need to submit to their authority for their ministry implies authority. And such authority is given by the Head of the body. Any member who strives against the mouth or the eyes of the body of Christ is striving against the ministry set up by the Head. For in reality insubjection to these members is insubjection to the Head. Insubjection is first expressed in many words, then in many thoughts. Yet the simpler we are the more we shall be united. This does not mean to say that in submitting to others you yourself have no ministry, since in the body of Christ we have authority towards one another.

Ministry is authority. In giving ministry, the Lord gives authority. As members of Christ's body, we need to learn not to be head. This is in fact the meaning of head covering. Head covering exhibits the fact that only the Lord is Head. And this therefore means that the responsible brothers themselves cannot decide on their own. A disciplined person has no pleasure in interfering with others' affairs. In order to exercise authority properly, he must learn not to take pleasure in meddling in the business of others. For God himself never interferes with or forces people.

Before the fall, the entrance to or exit from the Garden of Eden was never barred to man. Hell has no hedge, which means that people can quite easily fall into hell if that is their wish, since many are the roads which lead to destruction. Today twentieth-century man knows how to install a security fence charged with twenty, sixty, or more volts of electricity. But our God never interferes with, compels or prevents anybody. All who are naturally busybodies seeking to impose their will on others must be dealt with, otherwise they can never represent authority. The delegated authority is one who lets people know that he takes no delight in probing into another's affairs. To the contrary, the only reason he must speak is because he has received authority from the Head of the Church. One who has been taught does not offer his opinion casually.

Which chapter in the New Testament reveals the depth of a man's experience? It is unquestionably 1 Corinthians 7. There Paul said in one breath, "I have no commandment of the Lord" (v.25); yet not many verses later he said this: "I think that I also have the Spirit of God" (v.40)! In the same passage Paul also said, "I give my judgment"; yet it was "as one that hath obtained mercy of the Lord to be trustworthy" (v.25). Since he had received much dealing on many things, Paul was able to apply the same principles to other matters. He had followed the Lord for many years and had learned much; therefore he had arrived at the point of knowing the heart of God.

Both Abraham and Enoch walked closely with God. They therefore knew the way of God. It was not necessary for God to speak to them; they could know His heart. How strange for a person who has followed the Lord for many years to not know the pace, the direction and the way of the Lord?

We ourselves need to be instructed and disciplined. Only those who do not speak carelessly and who do not offer opinion casually can begin to be representatives of God, who is the Head. These also can begin to lead brothers and sisters on the way ahead. God will never delegate authority to those who are naturally critical. To be in subjection, you must be one who refuses to be head. Then as soon as anybody raises his head, you will immediately sense it as though you were shocked by electricity. You will know because having been judged before, you are sensitive to any similar situation. A brother who has been dealt with both in speech and in learning not to be head should have no trouble in exercising authority. All who have any problem with these two things cannot know the body of Christ.

Body Consciousness

What is the Church? So far as outward appearance is concerned, the Church is local. What are the content and life of the Church? If a group of believers does not stand on the ground of the local church,

it basically is not a church. But if a local church subjects itself to the authority of the Head, it naturally is
a church. In the church, we are members one to another, which means that no one keeps anything for
himself. Our heart desire is to fellowship with all the
children of God; that is to say, with all the members
of the body of Christ. Just as our personal experience
of the Head should be absolute, so our consciousness
of the body should also be absolute. The body has its
consciousness. This consciousness causes a member
to submit to the authority of the Head as well as enables him to be open to the body for fellowship. This
is called body consciousness.

As we have indicated, in natural appearance the
church takes locality as its boundary. In its inner content, it takes the Head as authority and all the saints
as one in Christ. The local church is not just a matter
of locality, it also bears the testimony of the body
which is holding fast the Head.

When I am in fellowship with all the children of
God, I will not be tempted to criticize other members. So, the basic requirement lies in producing in
our hearts a body consciousness.

What is the turning point from our not having
body consciousness to having body consciousness? In
much of spiritual reality we need to know both the
positive and the negative sides. It is not enough just
to know the positive, there is need to know also the
negative, else we will fail to learn a thing well. For example: The negative side of forgiveness is sin. The
opposite of justification is ungodliness. The contrast
to salvation is the world. In other words: To know

forgiveness, we need to know sin. To be justified, we must be delivered from ungodliness. To be saved, we should be aware of the world. (The Bible seldom speaks of being saved from hell; it speaks mostly of our being saved from the world.) We see, then, that many of the truths in Scripture are presented in pairs. If we mispair them, we bring in confusion.

Now the opposite of the body is individualism. So in order to see the body, we need to see first the negative—which is individualism. An individual must have some dealings with his self life before he can see the body. Many try to have dealings with such issues as loving the Lord and hearing the Lord. Yet the more they deal with *these* matters the more they establish themselves in their own righteousness, holiness and strength. And thus it becomes more difficult for them to unite with other people. It is much more difficult to call them to follow the footsteps of the flock.

We need to be taught by God in every area, including the area of individualism, for the latter lies in the deepest recess of man. Today people may come to see personal holiness, as is proclaimed in the Keswick movement; yet why is not corporate holiness emphasized as well? For the holiness in view in Hebrews 12 is *corporate* holiness. Many today are talking about personal faith. Yet why are we not stressing *corporate* faith too? The phrase in the Bible, "the faith," points to truth, whereas the word "faith" without the definite article preceding it means "a believing." "The faith" refers to the faith of the whole Church. The reason we are not paying attention to

Revive Thy Work

corporate faith and corporate holiness is because we are not aware of our littleness. If we saw our smallness as an individual member, we would see the much larger body; and therefore, we would see the corporate side of our walk with the Lord.

A piece of glass may retain a little water but it cannot contain a full cup of water. Each and every Christian has his portion of grace. But the individual Christian is not the whole body of Christ. Even if he receives *much* grace, he still can only be likened to a larger piece of glass that can retain a little more water. He is like a plane and not a cube. Today we need to lay aside our individualism. For what the Lord desires is not pieces of broken glass, but a glass cup. The principle of God to be followed is for "one [to] chase a thousand, and two [to] put ten thousand to flight" (Deut. 32.30). Today the Church is full of individuals. But if *two* (or more) should agree, they could put ten thousand to flight! The eight thousand overage is the excess gain. Today God wants the *Church* to preach the gospel and the *Church* to preach His word. Everything must be put into the Church.

The salvation we have through seeing the body is much fuller and richer than the salvation we initially experience. After one is touched by the revelation of the body, he can no longer say that it is well for him to just be a Christian individually. We need to let God do this work in us. For having body consciousness is not something arrived at or deduced by reason. Only as a person is being dealt with by God shall he see his body consciousness appear. He shall begin to understand that he is a member *in the body of Christ*. As he sees the sinfulness of individualism he will naturally submit to God. With such seeing, many problems shall be solved. It will not be hard for him to love, to live a life of faith, and to have prayers answered. Unless he sees the body, he is not able to work the work of God.

Any problem with body consciousness is the outcome of a problem with individualism. For a brother to be submissive, he must first set aside his opinion. Does not my hand listen to the words of my head my entire lifetime, and does it not always remain in its place without any murmuring? It causes no problem in my physical body at all. Indeed, were my heart to have another head (the hand), my body would be in conflict from dawn to dusk. So, too, would it be in the body of Christ. Hence individualism must be dealt away. We each must lower our heads and learn to be taught to speak, to think and to act.

Coordination does not depend on human thoughts and interests. If the coordination of our physical body is so good and well ordered, how much more should that of the body of Christ be? I believe in Christ coordinating His spiritual body. Its goodness and pleasantness and effectiveness are beyond our comprehension.

5 | Obeying the Authority of the Body*

How can we see and experience the authority of the body of Christ? The obedience of some members of Christ's body is selective. For each of us to practice obedience, the first thing to determine is, Who is above me? In the business world, the first question an employee will need to have answered is, Who is my immediate boss? If this is not clearly recognized, nothing can be done. Instead, there will be reprimand. There *will* be authority and there *must* be obedience. And this principle applies to companies and organizations. Unfortunately, too many imagine themselves as masters. Such people need to learn to obey. It is a lesson everybody must learn before God. In fact, all of us need to be disciplined to such a degree that we come to possess the very nature of obedience. And the result: everywhere we go we look for authority to obey.

---

*Delivered at Workers Meeting, Shanghai, 9 April 1948. —*Translator*

For example, the brothers and sisters who live in the church guest house should obey the authority there. At church meetings, brethren should sit where the usher has led them to. And while staying at someone's home, brethren need to obey the authority of that home, since each home has its authority. Christians need to discern who is in authority and to submit to it. All who pretend to be head know nothing of the position of the head in the body of Christ.

I have never seen a man who truly knows the Head who does not submit to Christ's delegated authority. Such a man never chooses wrongly in this matter of obedience. Any brother or sister who has never thought of learning to obey God's delegated authority falls into a very great deception. The Bible clearly declares: "the powers that be are ordained of God" (Rom. 13.1).

In Scripture, perhaps only a few places mention direct obedience to God; most relevant passages speak of submitting to man. Wherever we go, we need to practice obedience instead of voicing casual criticism. Many have not learned this lesson; consequently, they do not control their tempers and they destroy authority everywhere. These are disobedient ones. May the Lord have mercy upon us that we not be wild Christians. We should seek positively the object of obedience.

When I was in London our daily schedule was determined by the host: rising at six o'clock, lunch at twelve, and tea at three. One Swede who came from Japan shook his head and sighed. I asked him why he was so unhappy. He was fifteen years older than I.

He earned tens of thousands of pounds a year and had thousands of laborers under him. He told me he felt great uneasiness for he had been a student for some twenty-odd years. Staying now in the guest home whose host was not much educated, he felt most uncomfortable to have to be under the authority of such a person. It so happened that I remained in London for eighteen months. Had I not learned obedience, I too would have been criticizing and resisting; for like this Swede, how could I feel comfortable inside? Yet obedience is the very nature of the life of our Lord; and if we learn to obey God's authority, that becomes our protection.

Christians need to learn to be coordinated, yet coordination derives from obedience. An insubordinate and independent person is not and cannot be coordinated. Christians must learn to be in subjection to one another. There must not be any rebellious action or words of slander and criticism. Not only in the Church, that is to say, in the body of Christ, but even when one is alone, he needs to have the consciousness of authority. Let me say that we ought to learn obedience first in the Church, for it is much more difficult to learn obedience outside the Church. This is because, with God's life within us, it is quite natural for us to learn obedience in God's Church. And this serves as His protection against exposing ourselves. Yet in so learning obedience, we also rid ourselves of the spirit of Antichrist.

PART FOUR

THE RECOVERY OF BODY MINISTRY

1 | All Serve and the Recovery of Authority*

Today's difficulty lies in the unwillingness of the members of the body of Christ to receive supply. As members refuse to receive, all ministries are checked. When people have problems, they are not able to receive ready supply in the local assembly. They would rather go three miles away to obtain encouragement and supply. How can we speak in such a situation? We are not able to address even the fringe of their problems, let alone speak deeper and more open words to the brethren. Hence the need for today is for members of the body to put themselves under the authority of the Head. If they see the body they will not be hurt or stumbled.

In the past there were supplies in our midst, but these supplies could not be effective. Hereafter, we must ask for God's mercy.

Brothers and sisters must recognize especially the

*Delivered at Hardoon Road, Shanghai, 14 April 1948. —*Translator*

necessity of having authority in the local church. Romans 12 speaks of ministry; Ephesians 4 speaks of ministry too. But the ministry mentioned in these two passages is different the one from the other. Ephesians 4 speaks of the work of "the ministry" in *singular* number (v.12 KJV). This ministry is the same as the apostles' "prayer and . . . the ministry of the word" mentioned in Acts 6.4. For the particular ministry in the Ephesian letter is "the ministry" which is specific and unique and refers especially to the ministry of God's word. It includes among its ministers or laborers the four or five classes of gifted persons cited there. Thus not all participate in the ministry of God's word. Here the apostles, prophets, evangelists, shepherds and teachers have this ministry. Romans 12, however, gives an enumeration of many and varied ministries—indeed a plurality of them. All the children of God participate in the variety of ministries listed suggestively but by no means exhaustively in Romans 12. All the brothers and sisters in the local church take part in such varied ministries. In this case, therefore, each member must examine himself or herself and function according to the part given to each one by God.

Romans 12 begins with referencing the mercies of God as delineated from chapter 1 to chapter 11. Chapters 1-8 deal with sanctification; and chapters 9-11 can be encapsulated by the passage of chapter 9 that reads: "[God] saith to Moses, I will have mercy on whom I have mercy . . . So then it is not of him that willeth, nor of him that runneth, but of God that hath mercy" (vv. 15-16). And then chapter 12 follows up immediately with "the mercies of God" (v.1). Such mercies produce one result: consecration. And the purpose of consecration (as is made clear further on in this same opening verse) is for ministry, that is, for serving God; it is not for the purpose to produce preachers. Service is ministry, and ministry is service. Originally they are one word. This service is like the priestly service which figured in the Old Covenant period, as was alluded to by Paul in his first Corinthian letter: "they that minister about sacred things eat of the things of the temple, and they that wait upon the altar have their portion with the altar" (9.13).

It can be likened to the cook who prepares food in the kitchen but does not bring to the dining table the dishes he has prepared. This latter is instead the work of the waiter. Such is the picture of ministry. Ministry is to bring things to you from another place. Formerly you could not enjoy the food. Now, though, the one who serves brings the food to you so that you can enjoy it. On the one hand he who sows receives supply from the Head and on the other hand he passes on the supply to the brothers and sisters. A person's ministry comes from God. He receives this ministry for the sake of serving brothers and sisters—that is to say, for serving the Church, the body of Christ. Brothers and sisters serve together in a local church setting. Everyone contributes his or her share. No single ministry can serve in a representative way. What is mentioned in Acts 6, however, is a different story.

Today the supply of the local church is meager. The reasons are twofold: on the one side there are the works of the flesh; on the other side brothers and sisters have not learned well the lesson of obeying the authority of the church. In view of the flesh, the brothers in responsibility have dared not allow these fleshly ones to participate lest there be more destruction than construction. Thus, they help the one-talent people to bury their gifts. As a result, these people bring neither profit nor loss to the church. Their flesh is not brought in, but neither is their one talent brought in. Today, let us make a drastic turn. We cannot despise the one-talent brethren anymore; on the contrary, henceforth we want to gain these one-talent people. Naturally, when the one talent comes in, the flesh comes in too. But let us not be afraid of this dilemma. We shall address this matter in a moment when we discuss the recovery of authority in the local church.

What is the church? The church is where all the one-talent brethren are used. When all the brothers and sisters begin to function, the many one talents shall be utilized. That is the church. Today's need is not the ministry of the ministers (this there is no shortage of) but the ministry of the entire local church. Here there shall be not only the ministry of God's word; even more so, there shall be all kinds of services. Let us not bury the one-talent service.

Recover Authority and Deal with the Flesh

Authority needs to be recovered. Its recovery is necessary for dealing with the flesh. On the one side, all the brothers and sisters must rise up; though some may have only one talent, they still need to rise up.

On the other side, there must also be the recovery of authority; for this is because where all the one talents come in, there is bound to be flesh; and as flesh comes in, church authority is needed for it to be dealt with. Brethren should be told that such expression of the flesh is not right and will not be tolerated. Yet they should still be encouraged to participate. Otherwise, brethren will stop functioning and only a few will end up serving.

Everybody should have a part in service. No one should be allowed to be passive. We must reject the pastor system, for the single pastor arrangement is wrong; even a ten-pastor arrangement is wrong. There should not be one person, nor should there be only a few persons. Today, the one-talent problem must be dealt with. All those of one talent must come in with their service. There should not be one group serving and another group not serving. The local churches everywhere should inaugurate a turn-around. First, the fellow workers and responsible brothers need to be coordinated. Then, second, there will be strength to deal with the flesh in the church, to deal with rebellious and insubordinate brothers and sisters. And thus will the authority of the church be established. Five years from now you will understand what I am saying today.

In the local church the people need to learn to ask for instruction. Service is produced through asking. The emphasis in the church should not be on *doing* things, but in *learning* while doing. Each time something is done, the lesson of coordination must be learned. Learn to ask the church in all things. The brethren must not be opinionated but learn to obey. Those with ministry should speak responsibly, and also the rest of the brethren should lay aside their opinion in a responsible way. All need to learn to submit to Christ the Head.

In the church everything is under the authority of God. The responsible brothers need to learn how to give an order and the brothers and sisters must learn how to listen to an order. Those in responsibility must learn how to speak and how to be silent. Whether speaking or not speaking, they live under the authority of the Head. To live out church life demands our lives. The first and foremost thing to do is to obey. The brethren will bring a matter to the elders, and the elders will bring the same to God. Thus the brethren come to God through the elders, and likewise, through the latter, authority comes from God to the brethren.

Let those who are materially rich or who may have position in the world see and understand that the church does not beg for their service. They are asked to serve only in order that they themselves may be edified and perfected while performing their service. They should also be taught how to care for the poor in material things.

Recover Gospel Preaching by the Entire Church

In this matter of the gospel, we need to restore the preaching of it by the whole church. This is done not by advertising in the paper but by brothers and sisters going out to invite people in (see Luke 14.23).

There is a world of difference between personal invitation and invitation through advertisement. The whole church will rise up and serve. Such service is body ministry. We do not arrive at God's standard if only a few people are serving.

Today's way lies in authority plus galvanizing the one-talent services. Authority plus the one talents, and vice versa: that is the church. Whether a local church does well depends on how many of the one-talent brethren come forward. It is not enough simply to have the two-talents and the five-talents brethren. Our work is a failure if we are unable to bring in the one talents.

Nevertheless, let us be aware that the flesh follows closely on the heels of the one-talent service. Before you yourself as a worker learn submission, you are ignorant of any insubjection against you. But once you do learn submission, you immediately sense the presence of insubordination. If we who are responsible in the church are well coordinated, there will be authority in our midst. And with authority present, all rebellion and insubjection can be dealt with.

May I ask my fellow workers if you feel tired after having labored unceasingly? Perhaps God now wants us to let go. For the way for this day lies not in individual endeavor, but in body ministry and body action. The Church is a reservoir of Christ, that is to say, all the fullness of Christ dwells in the body (Eph. 1.23). If one day we see the entire local church preaching the gospel, how beautiful and how effective this will be.

Today there are few spiritual giants. A century

ago, with the Keswick movement, there were many. At that time people's knowledge of God's word was quite shallow. So that when an A. J. Pierson spoke, people found it hard to understand. Today our knowledge of the Bible has increased. Indeed, when someone begins to speak, we know more or less by his first words what he is going to discuss. Nowadays, a five-talent person such as Paul is most rare. Yet in spite of the rarity of such spiritual giants, the working together of a few one- and two-talent believers may well be equal to a Paul. Because there are so few Pauls, we must not wait for such spiritual giants to appear. We believe the time has arrived for the whole church to work, to save, and to preach the gospel. The way of the individual is over. Indeed, this is the day to follow the way of the body. We must be of one heart with God. We criticize denominations, and rightly so, denouncing their brand of sacerdotalism; but we are no different in principle from them if the service of the church is monopolized by a worker plus a few elders in the place of all the brothers and sisters laboring together.

Hence, as fellow workers our work today is not to work on behalf of the people, but to provoke *them* to work. Paul took Timothy into apprenticeship, and Timothy committed to other faithful men what he had learned from Paul (2 Tim. 2.2). These faithful ones then went out and energized more people. This is to be the way of our work today.

Heretofore we always worked for others: we worked till we contracted tuberculosis; it was all of no avail. Today's way is to instruct the brothers and sisters to serve. This alone will succeed.

If one person monopolizes the work, this discourages brothers and sisters to serve. Such a path is definitely wrong. Today's work of our fellow workers is to lead and help others to serve. Apportion to them the various services and let them do the work.

A deceased elderly brother once served in the navy. He told me that in firing the ship's gun the cannon shells had first to be transported from the storage at the bottom of the warship to the gunner's platform above in order for the gunner to shoot. The gunner himself did not go down to the storage to get the shells; not so. Now this elderly brother who told me this said that he served on this ship for many many years. Yet during that entire period he himself had never once fired a shot; rather, he was always helping others to shoot. Today we need to do the work, as it were, of transporting the spiritual "ammunition" to the brothers and sisters to let *them* do the "shooting."

One day we workers shall pass away, and the next generation will carry on. In readying the next generation we cannot train merely a few for service. We must help the *whole* church enter into service. If one day there is such a church that does all things together—in the edification of the saints as well as in the preaching of the gospel—then that day will be marked out as a most wonderful accomplishment of the church. Thus, the entire responsibility rests upon us. We must see to it that every brother and sister is serving. For everyone is a priest of God. Brothers and sisters may possibly bring in the flesh, yet they must still be allowed to function; but in so doing there will be the opportunity for their flesh to be dealt with. Some brothers may say to us, "But I have only a little, so I will not contribute my service." In response we must tell them, "No, you cannot be passive." It is so easy to bury the one talent. Many brothers and sisters are so frustrated by not knowing what is the right thing to do that they just give up. We must encourage them, however, to continue to serve. Believe me, this is the way. There will be such local churches in the near future. Then shall people see Philadelphia—the manifestation of genuine brotherly love.

Today's responsibility lies with us. God must first find His way in us workers, and then in the local churches as a whole. God wishes to recover the Church of Christ to her early state. He has been working ceaselessly from the Garden of Eden, next through the period of the tabernacle and the temple, onward, then, to the Church, and finally to the Holy City—the eternal dwelling place of God. At that time, Satan can intrude no more.

2 | Body Guidance and Body Ministry*

What is the connection between submitting to the authority in the body and submitting to God personally? What is the difference between personal guidance and group guidance?

The Roman Catholic Church and the Protestant Church belong to two different systems. In Protestantism each one is guided by his own free conscience. In Roman Catholicism all must accept absolutely the guidance of the Church. For it reckons that all God's guidance comes through the Church. In other words, people cannot approach God directly; they must go through the hierarchy of the Catholic Church to come to Him. Protestantism opposes such a concept. It confesses that all can follow God according to their free conscience. The Protestants reject Roman Catholicism, but they nonetheless bring in Sardis and pave the way for

---

*Delivered at Hardoon Road, Shanghai, 15 April 1948.—*Translator*

Laodicea (see again Rev. 2 and 3). Nevertheless, God calls His people to come out of Sardis (Protestantism) as well as out of Thyatira (Catholicism).

Personal guidance is based on inner life consciousness. The Bible speaks of guidance in two separate passages. One is in 1 John where it mentions the guidance of the Anointing (the Holy Spirit) (2.20,27). The other is in Hebrews where it speaks of the guidance of the New Covenant (8.8-12). The former stresses the recognition of spiritual consciousness; while the latter, the recognition of God's law. The New Covenant causes us to know the law of God, and the Anointing enables us to know the way of serving God. Unless one lives before God, he will not be able to understand His law. Nothing should be decided through outside rule. A decision made needs to be the response to inner life. The same principle applies to the Anointing in us. Not by outside instruction, but by the Spirit's anointing within. He will tell us what is of God and what is not of God.

We should be aware that these aspects of guidance are related only to our knowledge of God. They do not include other aspects. If we are so careless as to think that these guidances are all-inclusive, that is, to think that all instances of guidance must come directly from God, we will get ourselves into trouble. For both 1 John and Hebrews speak only of the guidance in knowing God. To know the guidance of our way in service we must go to the Book of Acts (see, for example, 16.6-10). The error of Catholicism lies in holding in her hand both the guidance to the Christian's way and the guidance to his personal life.

The guidance for our way leans heavily on group guidance. The Book of Acts is a guide to the way of our service to God and His Church. This, in fact, is one of the few books in the Bible which tells us how the Holy Spirit guides us in spiritual work. Thus Acts tells us that to some places the Lord permits us to go and do, while to some other places He does not give permission. In some instances there is mention of what the *Holy Spirit* says and directs. But in other instances it tells us how Titus and Timothy are sent by *others*. Now besides Acts, we find that the Letters of 1 and 2 Timothy and Titus are also Biblical books on work and service and they show us the same principle as is found in Acts. From these New Testament books we may see that there is a corporate side to guidance as well as a personal side. But corporate guidance plays the major part. When Peter stood up to preach on the Day of Pentecost, as recorded in Acts 2, the other eleven apostles stood up with him. What Peter said therefore became that which all of them said. He declared: "Repent ye, and be baptized every one of you in the name of Jesus Christ unto the remission of your sins" (v.38). Nobody afterwards said anything else. For example, we do not find John standing up and saying, "Peter, you should now leave some time for me to speak something."

Prior to Luther's day, the failure of the Roman Catholic Church lay in having given little or no place to individual conscience, little or no place for the reality of the Holy Spirit. The Church had become the sole and supreme arbiter of man's conscience. In the Protestant restoration, individual conscience was indeed recovered. But because its recovery lay primarily on the *individual* side, Protestantism has had to resort to meeting and voting to settle matters relating to corporate guidance concerning the way to labor for the Lord. True guidance of this sort, however, does not come through planning, consultation and resolution. It comes quite naturally without these human efforts. Where there is spiritual reality there will be no problems in guidance. True guidance derives from the unity of the Holy Spirit.

The Book of Acts at one point mentions the need of the newly-saved brethren in Samaria. So, the apostles in Jerusalem sent two of their number there to help them (see 8.14). Or again, when some brothers were praying in the church in Antioch, the Holy Spirit sent two from among them to go abroad to labor for the Lord (13.2). If it had been left up to us, we would probably have sat down to plan and consider how to go to Europe to work and serve God. But Acts shows us it is not by plan or consideration or resolution but through corporate guidance by the Spirit.

Even in the case of Paul's salvation, God spoke to him through the local church. Yes, indeed, the Lord spoke directly to him, but even more so He spoke through a member of the body of Christ (9.6,10ff.). Why did the Lord speak to Paul through another person? Here was Paul, a person so zealous in serving God by shedding the blood of believers. By this action he ignorantly thought he was serving God. One day, though, God shed great light upon him and turned his life around. Yet why did the Lord not speak exclusively directly to such a person? For we know from Acts that the Lord also spoke to him through another man—a believer in the church at Damascus. And interestingly, He did not even call on Peter, John or Philip for this task. Instead, the Lord called upon a little brother by the name of Ananias. This man had never been heard of before, nor was he ever to be heard of afterwards. The Lord sent a seemingly quite ordinary believer to speak to Paul. This incident dramatically illustrates the fact that guidance is in the body.

Whereas the ministry of the apostle John relates to the Family of God and that of the apostle Peter is concerned with the Kingdom of God, the ministry of Paul relates to the Church of God. And how did Paul's ministry begin? It began from the very day he was saved, for on that day Paul met up with a special feature of the spiritual life that is in Christ: the oneness that exists between the Lord and the Church: in other words, that the Head and the body are one and that the members of the body are also one (see Acts 7.58-60, 9.1-5). From the first day of his Christian walk Paul learned these two fundamental lessons. He saw and experienced on his first day in Christ the life of the body. This is why later on he could set himself aside and accept the work arrangement of the Church (Acts 15.22,25-27) as well as make arrangement in the work himself. This demonstrates to us that God's speaking today is not only to individuals but also to the body.

Today among us workers we would ask God to do this one thing: that there not be any guidance except the guidance of the body. The Lord's guidance in work is manifested through the body. If we practice individualism, we will miss God's guidance. Work and service are all in the corporate body. The work done on an individualistic basis is very different from the work done on a corporate basis. Moreover, individualistic work is fragmentary and is not related to God's movement. Working on an individualistic basis is either vain or false. Only by standing on the right ground will there be real work to do. Otherwise, all that is done will be vanity. A person may be busily occupied, but from God's viewpoint he may be very much at leisure. For not only doing nothing is deemed to be idling: in the eyes of the Lord, doing works which do not count is also reckoned to be idling. If I am busily occupied with my own things, this makes me an idler in God's sight. And hence what the Lord is doing I have no part in; and what I am doing the Lord does not count as anything. So that one can be very busy, indeed, and yet the Lord may pass him over.

Corporate Guidance Better Than Personal Guidance

In God's work we need to learn to accept guidance from others. This does not mean to say that today there is absolutely no individual guidance by the Lord, nor does it mean to say that instances of corporate guidance today cannot be wrong. It is impossible for corporate guidance to be absolutely without error. Sometimes there will be mistakes. But we as God's workers should ask ourselves this: If I have had personal guidance in my work, have I ever been wrong in such instances of guidance? I believe we shall have to acknowledge that it is possible for personal guidance to be wrong just as we must acknowledge that corporate guidance may be subject to error too. But in calculating the ratio, I believe we shall find that the decision of ten other spiritual believers is safer than my own decision. So let us learn this one thing before the Lord, which is, to learn to be a receiving vessel. Let us each learn to accept the judgment of my more spiritual brethren as constituting my own judgment. We must be able to accept another's decision as well as have others accept our decision. For the alternative may well be the following: Suppose a young worker does something wrong. You know this that he has done is wrong, and yet you dare not tell him because neither of you has learned this lesson. Thus, you allow him to continue in his error.

Sometimes a personal sensing of the Spirit's movement can be very deep and strong. Sometimes it may differ from corporate sensing. The sensing may indeed differ, but spirits must be the same. I want to do God's will; he too wants to do God's will; in fact all want to do God's will; and hence, there is no difference in the spirit. But if you murmur and get angry, your spirit is wrong as well as your sensing is wrong. Suppose, for example, you complain, Why out of all places am I asked to go to a certain locale to do God's work? Such a spirit is a wrong one. A wrong spirit will result in disaster. Let our spirits be right as well as be one.

The brethren having authority in the local church

must learn to pray together. The fundamental principle of church service is that the members be of one accord. The Bible does not teach majority rule. It teaches one heart and one mind. So let us gather the people together to pray. If there are people in the church who fast and pray, they will say the same thing. You yourself may have some thought, but in case you are not sure, it is profitable for you to submit to the body on the matter.

The church's spiritual course and the guidance of the Holy Spirit are closely related. Why do we need the leading of the body? Because with body leading we can avoid some unnecessary personal trials. *Without* the corporate leading it may take a brother ten years to find the way, but *with* the guidance of the body he can know it in a day's time. By accepting the judgment of the body he can save much time. The usefulness of authority in the church is in sparing God's children many errors along the way.

The principle of church service is to involve all the one-talent people. But as we said before, when the one talents come forth, the flesh will also be present. Hence for the local church to be a church, all the one-talent brethren must participate and authority must be exercised. Everyone needs to contribute, and everyone must obey. To have the exercise of authority but without the one-talent members' participation does not constitute the church. On the other hand, to have the one talents' contribution but without the practice of authority and submission will cause confusion. The problem with the church lies in not encouraging the one-talent saints to function, though in fact the church is composed *mostly* of such saints. The ruin of today's church is due to the burying of her one-talent members. If all the one talents come forward and all are obedient, the authority of the church is able to deal with the flesh.

Authority alone is empty; and to have only the one-talent people is confusion. But the presence together of both the one-talent factor and the exercise of authority constitutes the church. In obeying authority the fullness of authority comes to us. If people really know how to set aside their self life, there will be no problem in obedience.

The work of the Holy Spirit is in the body of Christ. 1 and 2 Timothy and also Acts all speak of the body and give intimations of the Spirit's movement therein. For instance, Paul said to Titus, "For this cause left I thee in Crete" (Titus 1.5). He also told Timothy, "Give diligence to come before winter" (2 Tim. 4.21). Here Paul did not ask them to seek in prayer for guidance. He himself told them directly where they should be and where they were to go and come. Today God moves forward by His Spirit through the body. Therefore, our work of service today must also follow the body.

In the beginning God planted a garden. There He went to find man (Gen. 3.8-9). After man sinned, God had no resting place on earth. Later, Noah's dove could not find any resting place for the sole of her feet on the earth that had come under God's judgment of the flood (8.9). Typologically speaking, God again had no resting place on earth. This is why later on God built the tabernacle as His dwelling place. It is then shifted from the tabernacle to the temple. But subsequently the temple, too, came under judgment: not a stone was left upon another in 70 a.d. This, though, was followed by the Church. For does not Ephesians 2 tell us that the Church is "a habitation of God in the Spirit" (v.22)? God does indeed dwell today in the Church, the body of Christ (1 Tim. 3.15). In the Old Testament period there was neither lamplight nor sunlight in the holiest of all, and yet the holiest place of all was full of light because God dwelt there. According to the same principle, today if anyone seeks to have light he must come to the church. You are unable to meet that much light in an individual saint; but when you come to the local church, you receive very much light. It will be strange indeed if you come to the church and receive no light at all. If people refuse to come to the body, they remain in darkness. But the moment they come to the church, they find light.

I would ask my fellow workers this: Where do you obtain more light on the Bible—in the church meeting or during your private study? From whence do you understand God's word more—from being in your room or from being at the foot of the pulpit? What one individual brother does not see clearly is made plain among ten brothers. Do you think your understanding comes from your mind? Have you really given due thought about it? Let us understand that all revelations come as light. With the light there is revelation (see Ps. 36.9). Today there is abundant light in the church. Consequently, we must recognize and acknowledge that to be an individual Christian does indeed have its shortcomings.

Body Ministry

The Church has been on the earth for a long time now. Yet God has never once asked anyone to manage a church, neither has He called upon a few more advanced brothers to set up a church. To the contrary, the services of the local church are all governed by the Holy Spirit. On our part, though, do we not sometimes reflect that the best choice for service ought to rest upon some brothers who exhibit good behavior plus have some gifts? But the situation seems not to be that ideal: those people possessing a good reputation often lack the necessary gifts, whereas those people whose character is not too seemly possess the needful gifts: and thus through the latter, people get saved; but in the case of the former, no one gets saved. It would thus seem that the Lord often works in a way which leaves us dumbfounded.

Today we not only cannot dictate the gifts, we cannot even pray for gifts. All is in the sovereign hand of the Holy Spirit (see 1 Cor. 12.11). Men can do nothing except submit to the Lord's will. If God wants to choose a Saul of Tarsus, He just chooses him. Nowadays, of course, we consider Paul to be a very beloved brother; but back in those days had we gone to Jerusalem to inquire about him, everybody we would have met would have appeared to have been afraid of Paul (Acts 9.26). Even people in Tarsus had been afraid of him. No one in those days would have ever thought that Saul could be saved, not even Saul himself! Today, therefore, we need to see the sovereignty of the Holy Spirit. All is in His hand. He who has not learned to obey the Spirit cannot serve well.

Paul did not receive authority by his having been sent out of men. Sending does not in itself bestow authority. It is the Holy Spirit who gives authority. Paul said to the Corinthians, "Ye are our epistle" (2 Cor. 3.2). Where there is gift, there is ministry; and where ministry is, there is authority. This is something beyond human striving. Having received the gift, Paul became a minister who had authority over all to whom he ministered. He therefore did not need any other epistle or letter of recommendation.

It is quite easy for us to say, "O Lord, You are the Head of the Church." For all works are in truth done by the Lord himself. He is the one who raises up the gifted. What those people in responsibility do is but to cooperate with the Lord. Today if anyone intends to do things on his own, he should be put under some discipline by the local church. Such discipline is for the purpose of dealing with the flesh. It is used to control the activity of the flesh. Whatever work done according to man's own thought should not intrude into the Church. The revival of the Church is not brought in by man's discipline but by the sovereign movement of the Holy Spirit. Without the sovereignty of the Spirit no measure of recommendation, appointment and sending is of any avail. The most it does is to add more seals or signatures to the letter of recommendation.

Today we must see that unless all the one-talent saints come forth to serve, the church has no future.

Priesthood is universal. This is the greatest recovery of the past hundred years. Many envision service as being done by only a few, but true service is done by the whole body (1 Peter 2.9). This, unfortunately, has not yet been fully recovered.

The Fall and Recovery of Priesthood

Those who serve God are called priests. In olden times they may have been involved in many services, but only one service was fundamental—to dwell in the holy temple of old. As we know, in the Old Testament times there was first the tabernacle and then the holy temple. In the latter there was a place set aside for the priests to dwell in. In the Psalms can be found seven or eight passages where dwelling in the house of the Lord is mentioned. The work of the priest was—and still is—to go to God for men and to go to men for God. God wants to be among men, to dwell with men, and to find rest among them. For this reason, there is need of the priesthood. Through the priesthood God obtains His resting place on earth.

Sanctuary and priesthood are God's double requirement. The work of the priests is to serve God. And sanctuary is the dwelling place of God as well as of the priests. Melchizidek was God's priest of old, but he was only an individual, so he was not able to satisfy the heart of God fully. What God has always desired is a *kingdom* of priests. For this purpose, therefore, He ultimately called out a people, the Israelites, brought them through the Red Sea, and had them enter the wilderness so as to make of them a kingdom of priests (Ex. 19.6). In the eyes of God His people and His priests were one and the same. As a matter of fact, He wished to have *all* Israel as priests: if they are My people, they are to be priests. This was why Moses as the mouthpiece for God said to Pharaoh, "Let my people go, that they may serve me" (Ex. 8.1, 9.1). All the people of Israel were to serve God. Everyone was to be a priest.

Now the law is the testimony of God. What the law requires is that which men should give to God. The law testifies for God. As to what God says to men, let men say the same to God. And the law had said that all the children of Israel were to become a kingdom of priests. But before the law had even reached the Israelites, when it was not yet even in Moses' hand, the children of Israel had fallen into worshiping the golden calf. So that after Moses had descended from the mountain and the presence of God, he commanded them as directed by God to slay their own brothers and sisters. The sons of Levi did according to the word of God through Moses and they slew about three thousand men. Hence God chose the tribe of Levi as priests (Ex. 32.1-29; Deut. 33.8-10). Originally all the Israelites were to have been a nation of priests. But now, from among the twelve tribes of Israel, only one tribe could be priests. Thereafter, apart from the tribe of Levi, no one had the authority to be a priest. We read in the Book of Judges that back then only people with money could engage a Levite to be their personal priest. We read elsewhere in the Old Testament that there was one king stricken with leprosy because he tried to be a priest; and he remained a leper till the day he died (see 2 Chron. 26.16-21). All who tried to serve according to their own ideas were overturned. For serving God is a position of authority and of privilege.

Nevertheless, what the children of Israel long ago forfeited has now been regained by the Church. Today God wants the Church to be a kingdom of priests. Declared the apostle Peter: "ye also, as living stones, are built up a spiritual house, to be a holy priesthood" (1 Peter 2.5). In the Book of Revelation we find the apostle John saying this: "he made us to be a kingdom, to be priests unto his God and Father" (Rev. 1.6). In the time of the Israelites gold and silver were to be earmarked for the temple and the tabernacle, not for the golden calf. The calf should certainly not be worshiped; but then, too, the *golden* calf must not be worshiped either. Today men need to learn to exercise the judgment of God to deal with the issue of the golden calf. Thus shall true service be produced and the true Levites come forth.

Today due to the insufficient understanding of our fellow workers, the work of God has been a huge failure. For example, though in the breaking of bread the saints know how to praise and pray, we nonetheless see that in service not all the brothers and sisters function as priests. The matter of service has not become universal. Moreover, though in the meeting all are able to sing (the priests in the sanctuary had also sung), we know that service is more than singing. Only when priesthood and God's children become one will there be the church. Today our service is done by three or five people, not by the entire con-

gregation. We have turned to be like the Jewish
nation of old, wherein only one tribe serves while the
remaining eleven tribes among us depend on the
numerically fewer Levites to carry out the service of
God. Apart from the few Levites among us, all others of us are adjudged unqualified to serve. Yet the
will of God today is for all the tribes—the whole body
of Christ—to serve.

Let me say to each of my beloved brethren in the
work, that notwithstanding how strong your ministry
may be, how rich may be your gift, and how useful
you are, you are a Nicolaitan if you monopolize all
services (cf. Rev. 2.6,15). You have nothing to boast
of; rather, you must confess your sin. Your personal
piety will destroy the church instead of building it up.
The right and correct way of work is to lead all the
brothers and sisters into service. More service or less
service is not the issue here. The pressing issue before
us is that everyone must *serve*. Unless all serve, there
is no church. Here, then, is today's way: the work
must be done by the entire local church; it is the
church, and not just a few individuals, that preaches
the gospel. No matter how well you each work, you
become a Nicolaitan if you are a substitute for other
people in the body of Christ. You may have a ministry
but you do not, as a consequence, have the church in
reality. However successful may be certain so-called
spiritual giants or great revivalists, their works are a
failure if they fail to bring in body ministry.

Today, preaching the gospel is to be our occupation. All other things are mere sideline issues. We
here and now make the gospel our focus. Our vari-

ous professions are for the sake of maintaining our livelihood. Our aim is for the gospel. Moreover, the gospel preaching is to be done by the entire body and not by only a few. Today's challenge is to universalize the service of gospel preaching; that is to say, all in the church must preach the good news. If brothers and sisters see the church as one body with its many members, then they cannot be individualistic anymore. The most blessed and happy event for us is to give our all for the gospel; and if that comes about, then there is no need to do much advertising or broadcasting. For all people will hear the gospel and witness the gospel in their very midst. They shall see that every saint is serving. If, for instance, there be three thousand saints, all three thousand shall work together for the Lord as one. All shall be serving.

How, then, are we to answer God's call? Formerly, people of long ago actually strove to gain the priesthood; now, though, priesthood is the portion of all God's people. Are we, in the end, to push it away from us? What the children of Israel had lost long ago can now be regained by us. Shall we today make worthless the service of God in our hands? Some may serve God as though saving His face and doing Him a favor, but we must see that being allowed to serve God is actually His favor to us. People who do not see the glory of God will count and recount the cost. But if they once see the glory of serving God, they shall climb up to Him and kneel before Him to serve. All who stand afar off do not know the grace of God. But all who know God's grace and know themselves will count no cost at all in serving Him.

3 | Body Ministry (1)*

Nowadays there is to be found a strange phenomenon among the children of God. It is as though there is but one class of people serving God. Yet the word of God makes clear that all who belong to God serve Him. When the children of Israel were in Egypt as slaves, they had no freedom. God delivered them out of Egypt and brought them through the Red Sea that they might serve Him in the wilderness (Ex. 3.18). As many as were under the blood of the passover lamb were those who were delivered and went out to the wilderness. As many of the people as were saved from the angel of death, just so, they were the ones who were called out by God to serve Him. In addition, as the children of Israel went out of Egypt they brought out with them gold and silver (12.35-36). Hence, as many as were redeemed were the very ones who were to serve God in the area of

---

*Delivered at Hardoon Road, Shanghai, 24 April 1948.—*Translator*

wealth and who were also to serve in the future tabernacle. In other words, service was not to be performed by just a few. Both in the Old Testament and in the New, we find that there was never the intention to make any distinction between people who serve and people who do not serve. No, it was always God's intent that all of His redeemed ones would serve Him. Only in fallen Israel and in fallen Christianity does there exist such a distinction.

God said clearly to the Israelites, "Ye shall be unto me a kingdom of priests, and a holy nation" (Ex. 19.6). Priests are those who wait upon God and follow after Him. No other class of people may approach Him as do the priests. Their vocation is to do nothing but serve God. And the children of Israel were to be nothing but a nation of priests. And hence, by definition, each and every one in the nation was to be a priest.

The priests ate, and lived, and slaughtered the sacrifices—all in the service of God. Their entire vocation was centered exclusively on serving Him. They might indeed do some other things, but these would be their avocations. They were to be there not as teachers, physicians, or other professionals—but as priests. Exodus 19 tells us that God meant to have all the Israelites, regardless whether young or old, male or female, to be priests.

The very purpose of God's salvation is for the obtaining of priests to himself (Rev. 1.5-6). The blood of the Paschal or Passover lamb delivered the children of Israel from the death angel for the sake of bringing into being a kingdom of priests. The highest calling is also the greatest grace by which men can be priests in the service of God. As many as were the people who exited Egypt, precisely that many were meant to be those who would worship and serve God. The very number of those who arrived at Mount Sinai was to be the very number who would serve God: no more, and certainly no less.

Sadly, however, at the foot of the mountain the children of Israel turned to worship the golden calf and thus sinned against God. Consequently, as commanded by God Moses ordered the people to slay their own brethren. The tribe of Levi alone among the twelve tribes hearkened to Moses' word and slew three thousand of their brethren (Ex. 32.1-29). The loss of these three thousand souls could not be compared with the much greater loss which the children of Israel would now suffer; for henceforth, they could not all be priests! Formerly, twelve tribes could be priests; hereafter only the tribe of Levi could (Num. 8.5-19). Originally, God's thought for Israel was a kingdom—a nation—of priests; now it became merely a tribe of priests. In obedience to God's word as delivered through Moses, the Levites had disregarded human affections and had stood on God's side in the moment of crisis. And thus, they obtained the exclusive privilege of priesthood. Here, then, we may notice one very significant fact: that most of the people had cast aside the priesthood of God: that due to idolatry, they had forfeited the priesthood. In short, they had engaged in other worship and service.

Later, in their striving for priesthood, the rebellious among the Israelites were swallowed up by the earth when it opened up its mouth (read Num. 16.1-33). To settle this issue of priesthood once and for all, God ordered the Israelites to lay up twelve rods before Him in the tent of the testimony, each rod representing a tribe and the rod of Aaron the Levite being among them. On the following day only the rod of Aaron for the tribe of Levi had budded. The rest of the rods were all dead (17.6-11). This thus served as dramatic confirmation of the fact that only one tribe had been chosen by God to serve Him. It further confirmed that by this time in the history of Israel, most of the people had lost their privilege of directly approaching God. If they now desired to come before Him, they had to consign this privilege to the priests. Even in the case of those among the eleven tribes who had a heart for God, they could only remain outside the tent of meeting. Thus, the eleven tribes were distant from God, while the twelfth—that of the Levites—was alone close to Him. The eleven tribes came to God indirectly, but the Levites approached Him directly. The eleven tribes were the served, whereas the Levites were the serving ones. In the record of the Book of Judges, we learn that the Levites were quite in demand in those days. Only after much searching could someone engage a Levite to come and serve in his home as priest. Even people with money could not serve; they had to ask Levites to serve God for them (see Judges 17).

Such a situation continued on for over fifteen hundred years. Of the twelve tribes of Israel, eleven remained outside the pale of God's presence, leaving but the one tribe of Levi inside. Not for hundreds and hundreds of years would this change till one day, in the New Testament period, Peter was moved by the Spirit of God to declare: "ye are . . . a royal priesthood" (1 Peter 2.9). All of the redeemed are now once again to serve God. Furthermore, around 95 a.d., and before he went to be with the Lord, John the apostle, in what proved to be the conclusion of the New Testament Canon, could also announce this: "he [Christ] made us to be a kingdom, to be priests unto his God and Father" (Rev. 1.6). Accordingly, the will of God for the Church today is that all are priests: even more so, we are to be a kingdom of priests. That which the children of Israel had forfeited is now, in God's good will, regained by the Church. Due to their unfaithfulness, the children of Israel lost the privilege of being a kingdom of priests; yet in this latter day God's will is for every Christian to be a priest.

Recovery of Universal Priesthood of Believers

Any service short of the service of a nation of priests is wrong. As a nation for God, the Church has been chosen out of the world; therefore, there should not be any further choice made in the Church. If there be neither the instance of sin nor fall nor golden calf, then God does not permit further separation. As many as are the redeemed by the Blood, just so, these many are they who are to serve. In other words, the number of sons redeemed back to God equals the exact number of servants whom God expects: the number in God's service is to be as broad as the number embraced by His salvation. Today there are only backsliders, for in God's eyes every single one is a servant or a maid. Today there are only the rebellious, yet there is no one who is not called to serve God. All services performed are to constitute the service of the entire local church together. This is what we have been talking about with respect to the "body ministry." Today's major problem lies precisely here. God is not satisfied with the service of ninety-nine percent of the Church. He wants everyone to serve. We do not believe in the majority serving, without the minority also serving. Nor do we believe in a few serving with the many not serving. Service is not the work of a few ministers. Why do we insist on *body* ministry? Because this ministry belongs to all the brothers and sisters.

The word of God tells us what we who know the mercy of God should do. But the current concept of Christianity is this: At the beginning I am saved through the grace of the Lord and by His blood. After a while, as I advance a little, I should forsake the world. Then sometime later, I should forsake all and serve God. Yet this is the teaching of fallen Christianity. According to God's word, however, the moment I am saved I am to enter in through the narrow gate, from whence I am called by the Lord to take up the cross (Matt. 7.13-14,16.24). Nothing is required if one is not a disciple. But in being a disciple, one must be absolute. To every saved person the Lord clearly places before him in advance the cost of discipleship. On the very first day of his salvation the

believer meets the tomb. On that very first day he
needs to forsake the world. We should not make the
gospel cheap, thus rendering it powerless. The Lord
never uses religious sales gimmicks to attract cus-
tomers. On the one hand the gospel *is* the cheapest
commodity; but on the other hand its cost is the highest—even the cost of Jesus' blood. We need to be
soundly saved. Only those who pay a cost can truly
rejoice.

When the rich young ruler returned home from
his encounter with the Lord Jesus, he still had his
money and his "great possessions" with him but he
had sorrow also (Matt 19.22). Where the grip of
money is, there is bound to be sorrow. When money
and its grip is gone, however, joy comes. Such kind of
salvation demands total abandonment. Today many
brothers and sisters are sorrowful like that young
ruler. In their hands they hold on to what they could
not lay down. Their only difference from the young
ruler is that they have not yet turned away since they
are still here meeting with the saints. To be joyful requires total consecration.

Last year I once asked a college student, "How
would you feel if somebody were to strike you on
your right cheek?" Most likely, the more you would
think about it the angrier you would become. Yet the
most hilarious person before the Lord is he who,
having had his right cheek smitten, has then turned
his left cheek to be struck also. He who has been
twice struck on the cheeks will be joyous and full of
praise. Let us understand that the way of the Lord is
absolute. A relative person cannot sing praises. We

do not invite people to come and serve, since all God's people *are* to serve. We only let you know that you are a God-serving person if you are one of His. God calls you to serve.

What *kind* of service is truly serving? Only body ministry is. As we have seen earlier, by definition being a Christian is to be a servant. So in order to have body ministry, there is the need for coordination of all the servant-Christians. What is coordination? It is not simply our being thrown together. To place my hand in the body at the latter's disposal is useful, but if it is left upstairs it is useless.

Upon anyone becoming a Christian, has he consulted the Lord about his occupation, dwelling place, and business? Is his occupation conducive to the gospel? Is the place he moves to helpful to his spiritual life? All brothers and sisters are fellow workers and must give their all for the gospel. All need to be coordinated in service. The Lord desires us to serve in this coordinated way.

We should therefore tell the younger brothers and sisters that whatever they shall do in the coming days—whether that be as physicians, teachers or other professionals—they must undertake them as avocations. This is because each one of us lives to serve God. They must also be encouraged to let go their wealth. And why do they need to offer up their wealth? Because with it, they cannot serve God. The Lord declares that no man can serve two masters. No one can serve together both God and mammon (wealth, riches, possessions) (Matt. 6.24). We all, like the colt, must be loosened for service (Matt. 21.2).

We all need to be freed from what ties us down in order to be able to serve.

Serving God the Highest Glory

When I was in England I heard that someone once sent one of brother C. A. Coates's books to the Queen of England and that the Queen was much helped after reading it. Now Coates had written eight books. So I asked the brothers and sisters in England why the person had not also sent the Queen the other seven books by Coates. They all fell silent as though I had said something wrong. Later I inquired and found out that the English people cannot just casually give books to their Monarch. The latter might not accept the books people send.

Consecration is the King of Heaven's favor to us, not our favor to Him. It is God who accepts our persons, being favorable to us in receiving that which we offer. It is not we who do God a favor; rather, it is God who does us a favor. In His mere acceptance of us, He is bestowing upon us a *great* favor. If I kneel before God and He sends down fire, this is His favor to me in accepting my service. Do not think that you humble yourself in offering to God. You may not realize that this is actually the mercy of God. Why, then, do you count the cost in serving God? You should learn to crawl on your knees into His presence in order to serve Him. Let us learn to bow before God and beg to be accepted into His service.

The blind today are not those who *cannot* see, but those who *do* not see. We are fearful lest we give

God too little, fearful lest He will not accept. Does our consecration profit God or profit us? Is it we who favor God or God who favors us? When we come before Him, our fear arises in our not being accepted. All who know God will say, "O Lord, here is something more." All who have met the Lord will gladly give half to the poor. The Lord said to rich Zacchaeus, "Today is salvation come to this house" (Luke 19.9). Today's problem lies in our not seeing the greatness of the Lord's salvation. Salvation is more than the saving of our souls. It means coming out of the former things. Let us recall the meaning of baptism. Why are we baptized? In baptism we declare that we have come out of this world and the things of this world. The issue of service is not resolved by asking three or five people to serve.

Today for the sake of the gospel we need the whole body to rise up and do the work of the gospel. We need to have our consecration renewed. What the Lord did in the first century must also be done today. We dare to believe in the first-century gospel; we dare to preach the first-century gospel; and we dare to do the first-century work. During that early period people could not freely preach the gospel and there were no church buildings to go to. People of the world believed in the gospel because they saw it portrayed right before their very eyes: they saw the Christians. In that very early time, Christians met in homes. But when for their faith they were burnt as torches, people heard them and saw them. The result of *seeing* the gospel far exceeds that of *hearing* it. For such a gospel shows that salvation is not a casual thing. The prayers of the martyrs became their gospel. In fact, history tells us that in the city of Rome the believers were at first killed but later the rest were exiled because of the tremendous public impact the martyrs were having!

Today Christianity has no power on others because it has no power upon us Christians. In the Church's early days people came to the meetings in spite of their fear. Today lukewarm Christians have little effect, whereas the testimony of the early believers frightened the spectators on the one hand but attracted them to such a gospel on the other.

Today we must bear all responsibilities. If the Lord cannot get through with us workers, how can He get through with the others in the churches? The Lord has been preparing us for the past twenty years and we have been waiting in prayer. Let us give to the Lord all our wealth, time and heart that He may have His way in us. This way will lead us to our destination. Let not money block our hearts, nor let it block the way of others to God. All brothers and sisters must participate in spiritual work. And thus this will provide the Lord a highway.

4 | Body Ministry (2)*

I believe God is going to do great things in our day. Indeed, He has already done great things for us. He has given us so great and so complete salvation. As He saved souls in the first century, so He saves souls today. As He saved in the first century to the uttermost, so He saves today to the uttermost. God will not change the gospel because of its two-thousand-year history. The demand and the result of the gospel remain the same. Do not think that though people in the first century had to pay a great cost in following the Lord, today we need not pay anything. As a matter of fact, people who follow the Lord today are required to pay just as much a cost as those of the first century. In those days, people had to forsake all; today this demand remains unchanged. Though there is a great difference between putting the lamp under the bushel and placing it on the lampstand, nevertheless the lamp itself has not changed.

*Delivered at Hardoon Road, Shanghai, 26 April 1948. —*Translator*

During the past two thousand years the gospel has not changed one whit. When the Church was born on that first day, God looked upon this newly created entity as being very good just as He had pronounced all things and man to be very good after His six days of creation had been concluded. Unfortunately, however, after a while this very good condition in both Church and creation began to change. Even so, no matter how much the changing condition, the original beauty of the first day remains the same in both: the beauty of the Church on the first day at Pentecost is the same as the beauty of Eve on the first day of man's creation. But we must acknowledge that like creation the Church has gradually changed for the worse. From Ephesus she gradually became Sardis (see again Rev. 2.1-3.6). But by the time of Martin Luther, God commenced the way of recovery step by step to bring the fallen Church back to God's original intent for her. So that during the past four hundred years God has done a work of recovery whose chief events can be traced as having happened about every fifty years. In the most recent hundred years, God has undertaken the work of recovery very intensely. It seems as though, in fact, that in just the last few decades recovery has well-nigh reached its peak. What the Church therefore possesses today is that which is the richest of all.

Body Testimony God's Last Recovery Work

We believe that what God wants to recover *today* is the hardest of all. That which we are most anxious about in our day is the implementation of Ephesians 4. Whenever we read John 3.16 there is no doubt in our hearts that it will be fulfilled. About this we have neither fear nor anxiety. Even if people should say there is no eternal life after one has believed and even if they should say there is no consequence after faith, I entertain no worry or fear about these matters. I have read the New Testament over two hundred times and therefore have no fear regarding John 3.16 and many other passages. I have read the Book of Revelation many hundreds of times, yet I am not even alarmed about its various passages. But I feel most apprehensive about Ephesians 4. I dread the possibility of its unfulfillment.

Ephesians 4 declares that the purpose of ministry is that the Church may arrive at the unity of the faith and full-grown maturity (vv.12-13). The Church is the body of Christ, and the Church is to build herself up in love. We are not concerned about the new heaven and the new earth, the lake of fire, and so forth. On the other hand, as I lie in bed, I often worry that Ephesians can never be fulfilled. I read and pray, and yet I have no confidence that the objective of Ephesians 4 can be fulfilled in today's Church. Presently there is such confusion and such divisions among the children of God; when, then, can they ever be one? Today there are such complexities in all kinds of ministry; how, then, can this chapter be adequately recovered? Such has been the content of my dire musings of the recent past.

But, my brothers and sisters, we believe one day God's recovery will arrive at this stated objective.

Ephesians 4 *will* be manifested. Today God is doing the work of recovery everywhere. Of His longstanding work of recovery, the last element to be recovered will probably be the testimony of the body. Currently God is causing us to see the beginning and to return to the earlier positive state.

Both 1 Corinthians 12 and Romans 12 show us that in the plan and arrangement of God there is not the substitution of one pastor or leader for the ministry of the body. Nor is there the dividing of God's people so that there is a group of brothers and sisters serving while another group of brothers and sisters are being served. In the word of God we see the universal priesthood of all the saints. The entire Church is a priesthood (1 Peter 2.5). God's thought for Israel was that she become a nation of priests (Ex. 19.6); though as it later turned out not many *were* priests. Today there is some progress in the churches everywhere. Brothers and sisters are free to pray, sing, preach, and take responsibility. But let us take note that what we have in our midst is still not the Church. For the Church is built on the universal priesthood of the *entire* body. The Church is not built on the service of a few brothers and sisters or even on the service of *many* brothers and sisters. *Without* a universal priesthood, we see the Roman Catholic or the Protestant Church. But *with* its universality, we see the *Church*. Let us acknowledge that serving God is not a matter of three or five, thirty or even fifty or a hundred people. Today *all* must serve.

In the days ahead it is not to be the ministry of the ministers but the ministry of the entire local church. In the past hundred years God raised up many spiritual giants who stood head and shoulders above the rest. From the 1820s to the present time an amazing number of such people were continually being raised up. Yet today we witness very few spiritual giants as though they no longer exist. For it is now to be the ministry of the Church and not the ministry of her limited number of ministers. It is not to be personal evangelism but church evangelism as the focus. It is the church preaching the gospel by the coordination of *all* her members.

Not only in the area of evangelism, but in that of instruction we also need to put the body to work. Formerly a larger number of converts used to cause a problem for us. When people were saved they needed to be instructed. Such instruction serves as spiritual education. Whether believers are educated or not makes a great difference. Now, though, we need *many* brothers and sisters to do the work of instructing new believers. Only thus shall the Church build herself up in love (Eph. 4.16).

So the issue now before us is whether we shall see the Church in reality. Three or five people serving do not constitute the local church. When all brothers and sisters in a locality are serving, there shall we see the church. It is quite possible for a group of brothers and sisters to give money to engage a pastor to serve for them. And thus from this you may conclude that the difference between that and body ministry is something quite small. But I say that the difference is vast. Body-working is far different from personal-working; and having all the brothers and sisters serving is also quite different from having just one minister serving.

The Way of Body Ministry

One—Engage All One-Talent Members

Formerly, we did have some new believers who were zealous in serving. But as they served, their flesh also came in. So when their flesh was checked, their service soon ceased. Giving such brethren an opportunity to serve created trouble for the churches; yet not allowing them to serve deactivated the churches: for when their flesh was silenced, their spirit too became silent. Such a situation was difficult to cope with. For this reason, authority must be recovered in the local church as well. On the one hand each must bring in his talent, but on the other hand the churches must exercise authority to deal with the flesh.

Today people long to have the five talents of a Paul. But we may have to wait for a hundred years before God will grant us such a great gift, such a great minister; or have to wait fifty years for a great teacher. Hence today's way lies in body ministry. Although one talent is not much, adding five one-talent servants together brings in five talents. Every redeemed person has at least one talent, with no one having less than one talent. So, in the local church you cannot find any member without a single talent except if he has buried it. Whether the body of Christ is going to be built depends on whether the one-talent saints are being built in together. We thank God if He should raise up the five talents. So far as the effect of the work is concerned, it is commendable to have the working together of great gifts such as those with five or two talents. Nevertheless, what we need today is to have all the one-talent folk come forth. This shall open the way for the Church and its work.

In this matter of service, brothers and sisters must learn to hearken and to accept the cross. As the Holy Spirit works, the cross will produce its effect on the human heart. On the other hand, the authority of the Church must be restored to deal with the flesh and all resistance to the cross. It is not enough to recover just the one talents or to recover just the authority of the Church. Both must be recovered together if the work of the Church is to be restored.

Two—Restore Church Authority to Deal with the Flesh

Brothers and sisters need to learn to hearken, otherwise the Church will become tumultuous. The young and the new believers are naturally ignorant of many things. They need to be admonished by the older and more advanced brothers and sisters to hearken. How very small we are! According to our nature, we will work when we are excited but will go to bed when we are unhappy. But now in the body, we must serve whether we are happy or unhappy, are in joy or in tears.

Three—All Committed, All Serving, All Obeying

If we are all committed and serving with obedience, the Church will soon experience its Pentecost. For with such commitment there will be coordination in service. We hope such a situation will appear all over the world. The foolish one looks at what he has in his hand; he does not see the world. Today we must enlarge our horizon to include the entire world.

Four—All Need to Be Trained

All the brothers and sisters in the body of Christ should receive training. What we need today is not theology but an education in the things of God. While the local assembly is young, brothers and sisters do not have much outlet. But if the local assembly is strong and spiritually rich, there will be much work to be done. Even with all the young people involved, there is still not enough manpower.

Five—Sent Out

After brothers and sisters have received training, they can be sent out. Many who read the Bible think that it was the twelve apostles who went out from Jerusalem to the ends of the earth. If so, how could twelve people cover the whole known world of that day? The Bible tells us that the twelve apostles remained in Jerusalem. Philip went to Samaria. Peter's visit to Samaria was most temporary. It would have been wrong for him to have stayed in Samaria. Gospel work is like a relay; it is not accomplished by only one person. All brethren need to receive Church training. At the same time the Church should also take care of the poor, the unbelievers, and the new believers in gaining them and educating them so as to send them out too. Such coordinated work is highly effective. Not just the apostles preach the gospel; all brothers and sisters preach the gospel. Philip was not called especially to be an evangelist, and Stephen was not particularly chosen to be a martyr. We imagine that only special brothers and sisters can do special works. But Philip was chosen to be one among the seven who served the tables (Acts 6.5). Therefore, remember that Samaria was taken for the Lord by one who was chosen to serve tables. Coordination requires all the saints to be consecrated and committed.

Perhaps some will say, I am not eloquent, I do not know how to preach the gospel. Today you need to learn. You must preach whether or not you can preach well. Perhaps the first time you go out, none will be saved. But the second time, some may be saved.

Six—The Professionals Give Their Wealth

In the Church every one must give his all. To the brothers and sisters who are in various professions let us say this: without offering your wealth to the Lord your consecration is vague, since no one can know if or when you withdraw your consecration. Scripture tells us this: "neither was there among them any that lacked: for as many as were possessors of lands or houses sold them, and brought the prices of the things that were sold, and laid them at the apostles feet" (Acts 4.34-35).

All Teachings Must Become Practical

Today all Christian teachings or understandings must become practices before God and man. They must become practical realities in our work with one another in the church and before a watching world. For example, Christ indeed said we are to be humble and to love. But though these are good, the Lord's work does not stop there, for He also wanted His disciples to wash one another's feet just as He had washed theirs (John 13.14-17). Today no one would confess that he is proud. Neither would anyone bring out a sign announcing that he is humble. Whether one is humble or not depends on his willingness to wash another's feet. This the Lord wants us to do just as He taught by both word and example. Teachings become real and firm through practices.

The Epistle of James declares: "If a brother or sister be naked and in lack of daily food, and one of you say unto them, Go in peace, be ye warmed and filled; and yet ye give them not the things needful to the body; what doth it profit?" (2.15-16) Agape love is unquestionably everlasting, but it serves no practical purpose unless it gives bread to the poor.

Suppose a brother has sinned against me. I should of course forgive him. Yet if this forgiveness remains merely inward, who can see my forgiveness even after doing so fifty or a hundred times? Forgiveness needs to be translated into practical expression.

The same is true with resisting the devil. If you only resist inwardly, you do not know the effect. But if you speak out in words, Satan will flee from you. Externalizing the inward can be most effective.

So it is with faith and baptism. After people believe in the Lord they should be baptized (see Mark 16.16). Believing in the heart is something invisible:

it takes a visible baptism to seal the faith. Believing with the heart is something nebulous, but being baptized with water is most practical and visible.

Let us similarly consider the matter of consecration. Mystical consecration is vague and obscure. Indeed, many consecrations stay in that realm. One may say to the Lord, I am willing to consecrate all; but the Gospel according to Luke shows how practical is Zacchaeus's consecration, for he laid all his wealth at the feet of Jesus (Luke 19.8). In these past hundred years the Church has witnessed many theoretical consecrations; but by contrast, consecration during the apostolic time was most visible and practical in its expression. At that time they settled all matters by giving their all. Today every brother or sister must submit to the authority in the church. He or she must also come with his or her time and wealth. According to 2 Corinthians God first receives "*you*" but then He receives "*yours*" (see 12.14).

All the brothers and sisters must take Christ as the center. Everything is for the gospel, everything is for service. We do not consider being Christian an avocation. In English there is a familiar saying: "professing Christian." But we each should be a "professional Christian," which means that we take Christ as our profession. The Lord demands us to deny ourselves for the sake of loving Him (Matt. 10.37-39). As was the Lord's demand in the first century, so is His demand today. In the word of God there is no half-and-half person when it comes to being a disciple of Christ; there is only the absolute person.

5 | Ministry and Authority*

Another point we need to see is the relationship between ministry and authority. The eye of the body has its ministry. It controls the power of seeing. If the other members of the body desire to see, they must depend on the ministry of the eye. The meaning of coordination in the body of Christ is that I give others what I have and others give me what they have. The primary condition of coordination is for me to accept my limitation, acknowledging that I am but a member, not the body. If I am an all-round individual, I become the entire body and will need no coordination with others. Yet I am but a member, so I cannot consider myself as having all. However important is the eye, it cannot substitute the ear. Color can only be distinguished by the eye, and sound can only be detected by the ear. Perhaps I can speak but I cannot walk. I need to depend on you for walking. As soon as we see this, we come to realize how truly lim-

*Delivered at Hardoon Road, Shanghai, 27 April 1948. —*Translator*

ited we each are personally. We have observed, however, that very few brothers and sisters really know coordination in practice.

For instance: the head covering of the sisters should speak to the brothers as well: yet frequently it does not. Christ declared: "I spake not from myself" (John 12.49). The Greek word *ek* used here means "out from." The Son cannot speak anything out from himself. In other words, Christ himself has His head covered before God. In turn the Church today has her head covered before Christ. And this reality of head covering is expressed through the head covering of the sisters. Whenever we are in coordination of the body, we each must lay down our head. It is not fitting for us to plan and to decide. Christ the sole Head is the one fit for such work. Yet how people today want to be the head. Let us therefore learn to resist our own ideas and opinions.

Concerning the interpretation of the Scriptures and the determination of doctrines, God has left for himself the teachers in the body of Christ. Today there are so many sects and so many strange teachings in the Church. It is because everybody wants to be a teacher. The fact of the matter is, however, that not all are, or even can be, teachers. In the human body, for example, what would be the use of the *ear* saying that a particular color is white? Whether it is white or not cannot be determined by what the ear does. The matter has to be evaluated by the *eye*. The many heresies in today's Church are the products of such confusion.

There is something most interesting to be seen in 1 Corinthians 12. Although eye and ear are both on the head, they themselves are not the head. In the physical body, it is the head that controls but it is the members which act. That which sees is in actuality not the eye, but the optic nerve in the head. Although in appearance the body seems to walk under the direction of the eye, it really walks according to the head. Today, a great gift in a big member of the body of Christ is altogether useless if it is not coordinated. We truly need to see our own limitation.

As we see the limitation of the members, the necessity of authority at once appears. If I am at odds with the members God has set in the body, I am actually at odds with the Head. If anyone is omnipotent and omniscient, he will not be in need of other members. In the Church we are not afraid of the ignorant, but we *are* fearful of the omniscient and the omnipotent. If we are ever to be coordinated, we cannot wish to be the head. Instead, we must wish to learn to hearken.

How does one know what his ministry is? It is best that we do not know. The Head knows your ministry, not you yourself. For this reason, we need to accept the judgment of the whole body. The knowledge of the body is dependable. Your own knowledge is not so trustworthy. It is in vain for any brother or sister to announce in the meeting that he or she has a certain ministry and usefulness. If he or she has that ministry, that person will be known in the exercising of the ministry. Hence, we feel with regard to the determination of ministry that the judgment of the group is more accurate than that of the person himself.

How are we to seek for spiritual gifts? 2 Corinthians deals with the difference between gift and ministry. The foundation for ministry rests on the death and life of Christ. Gifts are the powers the Holy Spirit has poured upon us outwardly. The Greek word for "death"—or, more accurately, "the putting to death"—that is found in 2 Corinthians 4.10ff. conveys the idea of a slaying. And thus it can be translated as "the killing or the slaying or the dying of Jesus." It so happened that when I was in London I told some brethren in the Western world that the original Greek word translated "dying" in 2 Corinthians 4 ought to be rendered in English with a new term: the "deathizing" of Jesus! For this death causes a person to die—to die to himself. What is actually being said here is that the slaying or putting to death of Jesus works positively in us. For what comes out of Jesus is a deathizing which puts you and me to death again and again in God's disciplining of us. Living ministry comes from God and it is produced by one dealing of God with us after another. Today the Lord desires us to serve the Church with ministry, not just with gifts.

As soon as a brother mounts the platform you know immediately whether he is a gifted brother or a brother with a ministry. In Southeast Asia people use a knife to cut or tap the rubber tree. Through the wound made by the knife the life of the tree flows forth. This daily event in the jungle can be used to illustrate a ministry in the body of Christ. After one has passed through woundings and fiery trials of every sort, he has life to impart to others. In order to have a strong Church, what is needed is not gifts but ministry of life. In a young church, spiritual gifts may manifest themselves in the beginning stages; but though there is much enthusiasm, there is not much life. On the other hand, you may see a brother who is not eloquent. You feel concerned and think of replacing him with someone else. Yet in him there is a ministry, for what he manifests is not gift but life. As the Church grows in stature, many ministers will be manifested; with the result that much life is supplied. Every brother should learn to discern the difference between ministry and gift. The Church needs to have many ministries raised up. A *young* church does indeed need gifted brothers, but we should not allow such a state to continue long. For gift is temporary, only ministry is lasting.

6 | The Coordination of Workers*

Is the coordination of workers governed exclusively by ministers of the body or is there any other governing factor? In coordination there is a certain measure of management, no doubt about it. Nevertheless, coordination is basically governed by the Holy Spirit. The Book of Acts has also been called the Acts of the Holy Spirit. It is so called because the Holy Spirit has supreme sovereignty. He is like the nerve system in the human body. It is true that the body of Christ is under the control of the Head, but the Head rules over the body through the Holy Spirit. Today the executive authority is in the hands of the Spirit by whom the Lord governs His body. Authority is not a thing, as though the Lord has given Peter a package of it which he may have refilled once the authority has been exhausted. Not so! For authority is the Lord himself. The authority upon Paul, John and Peter is all given by the Holy Spirit. It is the

_____
*Delivered at Hardoon Road, Shanghai, 17 April 1948. —*Translator*

Spirit who sets them in their various positions. The issue of authority is a matter of one's union with the Lord. The principle of having authority lies in being united with the Lord. In Acts 13 the Scripture makes clear that Barnabas and Paul were sent out by the Holy Spirit (vv.2,4). Whomever the Spirit chooses has authority.

A worker's personal work before God is according to his ministry in the body, but his movement in the work is according to the Holy Spirit.

Every Believer Must Receive Spiritual Education

In the past we passed up many opportunities to educate the brothers and sisters. They were born in our midst, yet they never came to know why we gathered together. To them our meeting was no different from any other. This is because we had not given them the right education.

Let it be known by all fellow workers that various basic lessons must be taught year round. Some in our midst have been saved for ten years, but they have never once confessed sin or made restitution. Now, though, we are preparing fifty-two subjects as basic lessons to be presented from year to year.* These subjects need little or no improvement. They only

---

*For further information about these lessons and their availability in English translation, see earlier in the present volume, Part Two, Chapter 1 ("Commencement and Continuance of Recovery"), in that chapter's subsection entitled "The Way before Us."—*Translator*

need to be taught year after year. Then, the foundation will be firm.

Teaching the gospel is different from preaching it. In preaching, variation is the norm. But in teaching, consistency is the way. In the preaching of the gospel no two persons use the same approach, just as no two personal testimonies are alike. However, after people get saved, the education they receive should be the same.

The kind of Christian one becomes depends much on the kind of education he receives. If we fail to spend time on this now, people will blame us later on. We need to walk in the same steps before we can have the same testimony.

In the process of presenting these lessons we must teach them in life; otherwise these subjects could turn dead. For we will only create more tradition if we fail to teach them in a living, anointed way. And in consequence we shall simply have one more thing which must be dealt with. But, if we teach these lessons livingly, people will sense life when not only hearing them for the first time but even after ten times.

Be Lowly and Remember the Poor

Beyond the above-mentioned matters, the local church should also look after the poor. No one serving God can hold tightly to his money bag. Every area of responsibility addressed by the early Church must be recovered. The abdication of responsibility in any one of these areas will incur great loss. Remembering the poor was one of the most important practices carried on by the early Church (Gal. 2.10). If we wish to know the heart of God we must recover this practice. Constant contact with the poor tends to enlarge one's heart. We ought to try every means to help them and to find opportunity to contact them. A church that isolates itself from the poor cannot be blessed. We should learn to condescend to those who are lowly (see Rom. 12.16), just as our Lord did in humbling himself (Phil. 2.5-8). Looking after the poor is more than simply giving them money. Looking after the poor educates you, enables you to touch something of the heart, and creates in you a wound. Such is the right spirit in caring for the poor. When I was in Shanghai one evening I invited a street lad to eat dumplings with me. We must always seek out opportunity to contact the poor. Around us there must certainly be those who are less well off than we are. When our Lord was on earth He never lost touch with the poor. Many have a wrong attitude that needs to be radically corrected. We must learn to stoop down and humble ourselves. The more people are saved among us, the more money needs to be sent out.

We can see in all of this that the body of Christ demands our life. When you listen to the teaching, you may perhaps at first nod your head in agreement. But if you put it into practice you will probably end up crying. Let us return to the principles established by God for His people. In so doing we will be blessed.

PART FIVE

DELIVERANCE FROM MAMMON

1 | Money and Occupation*

We believe the key to consecration is in God. But in order to solidify consecration, two conditions need to be fulfilled. The first element in consecration has to do with the Church. For consecration is not only committing ourselves to the Lord, it is also committing ourselves to the Church. Of course, consecration is presenting ourselves to the Lord, but nobody can tell when such consecration becomes problematic and is withdrawn. In case consecration is made under the authority of the Church, it can be preserved. Consecration without commitment to the Church is something fluid.

The second element in consecration has to do with money and occupation. Consecration without commitment to the Church is weak consecration; consecration without it touching money and occupation is superficial consecration.

---

*Delivered at Hardoon Road, Shanghai, 19 April 1948. —*Translator*

Money

How does God look upon money? Here we should understand two relationships. One is that between God and all creation. The other is that between creation and money. Out of one source God created all things. What the feet step on and the hands touch are all created by Him. God is not only the Creator of all things, He is also the Lord of all things. Satan is God's antagonist, but he has no way to deal with Him. Since he cannot possibly deal with God, he tries to deal with all things that come from God. In other words, he is not able to destroy God himself, so Satan turns to destroy the works of God if he can. If he can perhaps pluck God's created things out of His hand, he will gain the upper hand. So in trying to destroy God's work, Satan lays his hands on His creation.

Today I would like to show you the relationship between all things and money as well as the relationship of the created things to God. Satan desires to gain all things for himself, but he is not able to gain them one by one because each of them is just too much for him. The all things of which I have been speaking include oxen, sheep, trees, stars, and so on and so forth. Each is countless and beyond description. Now because God had created all things out of one source, so, Satan in turn has tried to reduce them all into one. And this one thing is *money*. There is nothing in the world that cannot be bought. With money, you can have all things. Hence, money is called "currency"—that is, that which has common acceptance. The value of a piece of rock and a piece of wood cannot be added up. Neither can the value of a chair and a table be added up. Satan therefore invents money by which to unify all things. He simplifies the "all things" of God through this ingenious arrangement of money. Out of one source comes forth the many shapes and forms of all things in the world. Accordingly, Satan attempts to reduce through money all things back into one. What things we see can all be calculated in terms of money. Money is therefore the means to unify them all. But though all things were created by God, money itself is not His creation. It belongs to Caesar. When the Lord was queried as to whether it was lawful to pay tribute to Caesar, He asked that a denarius coin be shown him. He then said, "Render . . . unto Caesar the things that are Caesar's" (Matt. 22.21). (It should be noticed, incidentally, that Jesus never carried money on His person, or else He would have been accused of having the things of Caesar in His pocket.)

No, money was never created by God, it was invented by Satan for the sake of unifying all things. Accordingly, the value of all things could now be computed in monetary terms. The earth was created by God, but today men can use money to calculate the value of the earth. If it were possible, man would even calculate the worth of the moon or of the hydrogen in the sun. Men can buy anything. They can buy time, even human souls. One brother I know has worked in the post office for decades; which means that the post office has bought him for those years. The property of Jacob included souls as well as oxen and sheep. Moreover, Revelation 18 tells us that "souls of men" are one of the kinds of merchandise listed there that was sold by the merchants of the earth (vv.12-13). Out of one, God created all things. Now, though, Satan attempts to gather them all back into one.

In gaining God, we obtain His all things. Satan, however, obtains them by gaining money; for is not money almighty, cannot money buy everything? We buy wood, stone, or any other item we would love to have. But to do so, money is needed. Mammon or money therefore becomes a power, even the center of men's worship (see Matt. 6.24). Whether men worship God or worship Mammon (the Aramaic term used by Jesus to personify money, wealth or earthly possessions) becomes the focal point of universal conflict. Worshiping God places us on one side of money—the side that *opposes* it, while worshiping Satan places us on the other side of money—the side which *worships* it. The opposite of God is Mammon. Why can Mammon stand in opposition to God? Because it alone can gather up all things. The love of money is more than a root of all evils (1 Tim 6.10); it is also idolatry, because money to many people is an idol. Interestingly, the Bible treats covetousness and idolatry as one sin (Col. 3.5; cf. Eph 5.5). A person who is unclear about money is not soundly saved. We know we cannot baptize a person who still has an idol in his home. Yet many saved ones have not clearly dealt with the issue of money, it remaining for them an idol. We often hear it said that India is a nation of idols because the country has more of them than people. Yet how many more are there who worship Mammon than there are who worship these other kinds of idols? From Asia to Africa, from scientists to the superstitious—all, it seems, worship Mammon. Mammon is most commonly worshiped.

God wants to lay hold of us; Mammon too wants to lay hold of us. Unless God's people are delivered from its influence, they have no testimony nor can they be good Christians. How can one serve the Lord if he holds on to two opposites? Why is it that the Lord demanded so strictly of the young ruler that he sell all? That young man was quite good and law-abiding. But the Lord said, "one thing thou lackest yet" (Luke 18.18-23). And that thing, which was the most important thing in his life, centered around the issue of wealth and how he needed to be delivered from its hold on him. On the other hand, we find that at the conversion of Zacchaeus, the latter promised to give half of his goods to the poor (19.8). This principle is the same that is seen in the letter of Paul to the Corinthian believers where he is found quoting from the Old Testament: "He that gathered much had nothing over; and he that gathered little had no lack" (2 Cor. 8.15).

In Church history the Moravian Church has been the most powerful missionary church. Their founder Count von Zinzendorf offered all his estate to the Lord. Sister Eva also gave her all. Several decades ago, the now famous Cambridge Seven came to China to preach the gospel. Among them was C. T. Studd, the renowned cricketeer of England. His inheritance had amounted to two hundred thousand

English pounds. He proposed to give it all away. At the same time he told the British Foreign Ministry that he wanted to go to China as a missionary. The consul was amazed at his consecration and dared not accept his application. After an entire week had gone by, Studd still had no change of mind about going to China and gave away all his inheritance. God was able to use Studd greatly because he had overcome the Power of Money. Because Mammon stands against God, every child of His needs to overcome its pervasive power. If the power of Mammon is not overcome, there will be no spiritual power. Yet please note that the power of Mammon does not derive from the *amount* of money or possessions, for this idol may exert an even stronger power upon the poor than upon the rich!

For this reason, a Christian should work not for the sake of having or accumulating money but to make a living for himself and his family. It is obviously not right to earn money *un*righteously, but can we say earning *righteously* is altogether right? *For money itself is unrighteous.* This is made quite clear in Luke 16: "Make to yourselves friends by means of the mammon of unrighteousness" (v.9). Money is unrighteous because its very nature is opposite to God's. Let us see clearly the position of money, or else we shall find it quite hard to be a Christian. Christians cannot take advantage of worldly people's money. If we do, we lose our Christian status. We testify to the fact that our Father is above all and that we are His children. How can people such as we are make a profit at the expense of even the people of the world?

It is below our dignity. Speaking from the Christian viewpoint, in the entire world there are but two classes of people: the unbelievers and the brethren. And if it is true that we cannot disadvantage the unbelievers, can we at all do so to our Christian brethren? Let us therefore solve this problem well. A Christian does not work for the sake of having or accumulating money, he works to maintain a living.

Occupation*

Occupation is the second issue before us. What is the occupation ordained of God? That which He has

---

*The reader is urged to consult the chapter entitled "Occupation" that appears in Watchman Nee, *The Spirit of Judgment* (New York: Christian Fellowship Publishers, 1984), 79-94. It is the text of a message the author delivered just a few months later on the same subject. There, however, he gives a much fuller and more thorough presentation of his ideas and conclusions than he has only briefly outlined in the pages of this and the chapter to follow that are now before the reader. Nevertheless, it bears repeating here the observations which the present translator made as an introductory footnote to the fuller treatment on "Occupation" just referenced: "This message when given in [the summer of] 1948 at the Mount Kuling Conference Center near Foochow, China was a timely one, in view of a special situation then existing in China which seriously needed to be addressed on behalf of the Christians there. The same, however, may not be entirely or even partially applicable to the believers living within Western social and economic systems. The reader himself must judge. Yet the underlying principle advanced by the author in this message is nonetheless worthy of consideration; for although economic systems may indeed differ and local situations may doubtless vary, the basic points enunciated here can be of great help to those who seek to be led by the Spirit of God in choosing their occupations." —*Translator* prescribed for men is this: that "in the sweat of thy face shalt thou eat bread" (Gen. 3.19). In the Old Testament we learn that God had appointed Adam to till the ground and Abel to keep the sheep. Abraham and Jacob were also shepherds. And Genesis 4 mentions the forger, the maker of every cutting instrument of brass and iron. All these are works of labor. In the New Testament we find that the apostles were fishermen, and Paul was a tentmaker (Acts 18.3). These too are works of labor.

Paul said, "Now to him that worketh, the [wage] is not reckoned as [a favor], but as [what is due]" (Rom. 4.4). Occupations involving labor do not have the element of profiteering in them; therefore, they are legitimate. Increasing the price of that which increases in value cannot be considered profiteering since it is the result of selling one's labor.

Suppose there are ten thousand sheep in the world. Through my shepherding the number is increased to eleven thousand. Thus my labor causes an increase of one thousand sheep in the world. This is the increase of value. Or suppose there is but one grain of wheat. Through my cultivation it becomes thirty or even one hundred grains. This too is the increase of value. I should therefore gain in money because by my labor I have caused an increase of ninety-nine additional grains of wheat in the world. Or consider another example. Paul purchased cloth and sewed the same into a tent in the evening. He sold it the next day. Now the money he gained came through the work of sewing. But suppose you buy five rolls of cloth and simply sit around waiting for their price to rise before you sell them; let me say that you have not added one inch to the cloth and yet you earn money out of them. Such an occupation should be avoided. Any occupation which does not increase value needs to be changed. We must reform our conception of labor and occupation. Instead of going after profit, we need to aim at engaging in occupations which increase the value.

We should not be engaged in works which do not increase value. Receiving wages from our labor is proper. But an occupation which does not increase value may not only corrupt our heart, it may affect our testimony before God and Satan. We must be delivered from money. Our occupation should be related to either works of labor or to the increase of value. We shall be useful in the service of God if we are clear in our occupation. Let us expand our view. No one can serve God on the one hand and hold on tightly to money on the other. May we offer both our selves and our occupation to God for the fulfillment of His purpose.

The Church and Money Matters: in Special and Ordinary Times

In times of revival the Church needs to adopt temporary measures, those which are different from long-term measures. During a period of revival everything must follow the spontaneous leading of the Holy Spirit; but over the long term there should be Church arrangement. In the days of revival Ananias should not have kept back something for himself. Yet having done so, he lied and sinned against the Holy Spirit (Acts 5.1-5). But Paul in one of his letters said this: "if any provideth not for his own, and specially his own household, he hath denied the faith, and is worse than an unbeliever" (1 Tim. 5.8); he further wrote this in the same letter: "If any woman that believeth hath [dependent] widows, let her relieve [assist] them, and let not the church be burdened; that it may relieve [assist] them that are widows indeed" (v.16). We do not expect what is done during revival to be the same as what is done in ordinary days. At times of revival we cannot rest without giving our all. But over the long term we must take care of our families, especially when the children are small. To gather more is not wrong, but to keep more *is* wrong. Let us tighten our living standard so as to be able to set aside money for the purpose of helping others. Those who have given know that "it is more blessed to give than to receive" (Acts 20.35).

Let me say again that the way the Church manages money in ordinary times is different from her way during times of revival. During the latter, we cannot quench the moving of the Holy Spirit. But for the ordinary or extended periods of time, the Church must make certain arrangements.

In Money Be Wise Stewards of the Lord

We offer our all to the Lord. What we receive back from Him is very much different from what we had owned before. Formerly we were owners and masters; now we are stewards. Stewards who waste their Lord's money will be accused (Luke 16.1). Today the living standard of each saint is not the same, but the common principle to be frugal applies to all.

As soon as the issue of money is settled, the person is enlarged. Today, due to our differing backgrounds the same word stirs up different thoughts. For example, if I invite a person to a meal in my home, a northern Chinese would expect wheat bread at the table whereas a southerner would expect rice. In like manner, different people entertain different ideas about the needs of the Church and their solution. Nevertheless, we must not stand on our own ground; rather, let us see things from God's perspective. And God has made clear that no one can serve two masters. Declared the Lord Jesus: "You cannot serve God and mammon" (Matt. 6.24). The reason why we are in darkness has much to do with our relationship to money (vv.21-23). But with the money issue settled, light shines forth, making it possible for many other matters in our lives to be resolved.

The gospel is like water in a bottle, and money or wealth is like the cap of the bottle. Unless your money is released the gospel cannot be discharged. Without the sending out of money one does not even know how to be a normal person. How can you see if your eyes are blinded by the bright glint of gold? Except you are liberated from Mammon, you cannot see the Lord.

2 | Dealing with Mammon and Serving God*

There are really only two ways of service for mankind: either a person serves God or serves Mammon (Matt. 6.24). Probably eighty percent of the Christians in the world are serving Mammon, and perhaps eighteen percent are serving Mammon as well as serving God. It is extremely difficult to find a few who serve God exclusively. Formerly, we avoided mentioning money and wealth. This was due on the one hand to our unfaithfulness and to the difficulty of talking about it on the other. As was intimated before, money is itself unrighteous (see Luke 16.9 again). Christians will obviously not be serving God if they should earn money by illegal or unrighteous means; yet even earning money in righteous ways may not be serving God. For the Christian, profiteering itself is illegitimate. Unless one has settled this critical issue in his Christian life there shall be many unresolved problems. As we pointed out earlier, out

---

*Delivered at Shanghai, 20 April 1948. —*Translator*

of one origin God had created all things, but God's enemy has used money to reunite all things into one. God made all things, but money can buy all things. Any thought of profiteering, if carried out, is therefore in the service of Mammon.

Biblically Acceptable Occupations*

All legitimate occupations seek gains from nature, not from people. For example, suppose there are two billion people in the world, and each one has a dollar in his or her pocket and nothing more elsewhere. The total amount of money in the world is therefore two billion dollars. To increase the money in my pocket I must take it from the pockets of other people. How can a Christian take money out of others' pockets and put it into his own pocket? Is it not beneath the dignity of a child of God? Hence what we must do is to increase the value of nature.

All the occupations of God's people cited in the Bible are related to nature. Fishing, for instance, is taking in the produce of the sea. Farming is taking in the produce of the land. Such professions may increase my money without lessening another's. We may increase our own money, but we should not decrease another's. The increase of Abraham's and Isaac's herds and flocks was God's blessing upon His servants (Gen. 24.35, 26.12-14), but the increase of

---

*Before proceeding further, the reader is advised to read again an important explanatory note which appears in the section of the preceding chapter of the present work that deals with the same subject on occupations. —*Translator*

Jacob's herds and flocks was stealthily gained at Laban's expense (30.31-43). Abraham's increase was right, while Jacob's increase was wrong, for the latter sinned against Laban in such activity. Today, many there be who are like Jacob. How can we serve our God well if we have not settled this issue? We should resist works in the realm of pure commerce.

The King of Tyre mentioned in Ezekiel 28 points to Satan. He fell by the abundance of his traffic, and traffic there has reference to pure commerce (see Eze. 27). Ezekiel 27-28 marks the earliest commerce while Revelation 18 marks the last. Ezekiel 27-28 is the beginning of world commerce whereas Revelation 18 represents its conclusion, with its prominent mention of the "merchants of the earth." At the end time the Antichrist will do business through Babylon. Pure commerce represents more than a matter of acquiring or earning money; there is also the issue about it as to just how money is actually acquired. Today we cannot but pay attention to the matter of how money is gained. We may increase our own, but we should not cause society to suffer loss. Refining iron and transforming it into steel, for instance, gives increase to society. Such an occupation is acceptable.

Today our thoughts need to be disciplined by God. The profiteers see nothing else but money. They look not at how many fishes they have but only at how much money they can acquire. The Jews were originally occupied in farming, pasturing and laboring, for in Old Testament times God had distributed land to the children of Israel that each might work on his own land. Here the Jews learned a lesson. But after their fall and dispersion, they have become some of the biggest merchants in the world. This becomes a stronghold that is very hard to break through since pure commerce is such a great temptation. How we all need to do an about-face in regard to it. May God transform our thought.

Unrighteous Steward and Unrighteous Mammon

Luke 16 speaks of the unrighteous steward and unrighteous mammon or money. Here the master commends the steward for his cleverness in using his master's money to make friends for himself. This parable can be divided into two parts: the story itself, followed by the teaching deduced. Verses 1-7 tell the story; from verse 8 onward is the teaching: "the sons of this world are for their own generation wiser than the sons of the light." For the unrighteous steward changes a hundred measures of oil to fifty and a hundred measures of wheat to eighty. Such economic activities are unrighteous in their procedure. They naturally are to be condemned. But in the following verses we see that the Lord calls us to save people to the eternal tabernacle by means of the mammon or money of unrighteousness. The mammon itself as well as its procedure are all unrighteous. Hence, the story itself speaks of the unrighteous procedure, whereas the teaching part tells of the unrighteous mammon.

The story does not refer to the oil or the wheat as being unrighteous. It declares from the outset that the *man* is unrighteous—he is called by the Lord an unrighteous steward. Yet in the teaching, even *money* is labeled as being unrighteous: Jesus termed it the mammon of unrighteousness or unrighteous money. On the basis of this passage some deem money to be right because it is said that money can be used to make friends and send people to the eternal tabernacle. But we need to understand that before God the very nature of money is unrighteous. We need to repent of our concept of money. For God and money stand opposite to each other. How can we allow anything to stand in opposition to God? So we serve either God or Mammon. Mammon desires men's worship as much as God desires men's worship. Let us therefore have this issue of money resolved in our Christian lives; and if so, then we shall discover that the way to serve God is made easy.

When the children of Israel came out of Egypt, they were given permission by the Egyptians to remove the latters' gold, silver and jewelry; and the more they took out the better (see Ex. 12.35-36). If today the money we have comes by way of righteous means, we can take more. But if it is obtained by *un*righteous means, it needs to be returned. Yet some will find it difficult to let go once the money is in their hands. Nevertheless, let us preserve the dignity of our being Christians.

3 | Deliverance from Mammon*

The Bible places the idolatry of Mammon fairly high. It stands in opposition to God. Today there are far more people who are captured by Mammon than are captured by God. Perhaps eighty percent are taken in by it. Of the remaining twenty percent, probably eighteen or nineteen percent serve both God *and* Mammon. It is very difficult to find one among a hundred people who truly serves God. In short, Mammon wins many more souls than does God.

As we deal afresh with this matter of body life, we are continually being confronted with not only the difficulty of individualism but also that of mammon or money. Individualism hinders our serving God, but so does money. The moment a person serves it, he cannot serve God either personally or corporately. We may even say that deliverance from Mammon is perhaps the primary basic requirement in

---

*Delivered at Hardoon Road, Shanghai, 27 April 1948. —*Translator*

serving God. Unless one is truly delivered from such idolatry, he is unable to serve God.

To recapitulate what was said earlier, all things have been created by God who is the sole source of all things. He is also above all things (see Acts 17.24-25). As men witness these created things all about them, they worship God. It is therefore wrong and foolish for the human mind to invent atheism. The things in the heavens and the earth lead us to the knowledge of God (Rom. 1.20). Yet because all these things are so varied and complex, God's enemy Satan attempts to unite them into one, for he recognizes how impossible it is to sum up so many different things in God's creation. For example, a chair and table do not add up. Moreover, what can possibly be the sum total of a grown-up man, a child, a load of luggage, a bar of gold and a piece of land? But if all can be valued in terms of money, they become statistically possible to be totaled up. If all things are not unified in this manner, how can business people ever balance their budgets? Or how can they intelligently compute when there are so many diverse and complicated units? Money alone can make it possible to calculate all things. With the invention of money by God's adversary, land is no longer land—but money; rice is no longer rice—but money; electricity is no longer elctricity—but money. According to Revelation 18, even souls can be calculated and sold in terms of monetary value (v.13). When people sell their time they are actually selling themselves. For example, when we employ laborers we promise to pay them such and such for so many hours of work.

In a sense, is this not using money to buy souls? Money can purchase souls as well as purchase all created things. God created the earth, and men have cut it into pieces, using money as the means for determining the value of each piece of land. When men eventually reach the moon they will no doubt sell it for money also! If airplanes fly through my territory, it is required of the airplane company to pay for the relevant air rights. Today we take this for granted, but according to the Bible this is rather unusual. We know that in six days God created all things. Can you calculate how much they are worth? There are so many things in so many forms, shapes, and colors. But today Satan simplifies and unifies them all on the basis of money.

Moreover, money controls all things. God on the one side created all things, but Satan on the other side turns all things into monetary value and unifies them all. With money man can now purchase anything. He can purchase gold, purchase furniture, even purchase China. There is nothing which cannot be bought. Mammon stands in opposition to God. This is why the Scripture not only declares that "the love of money is a root of all kinds of evil" (1 Tim. 6.10), it also joins covetousness and idolatry together (Eph. 5.5, Col. 3.5). Covetousness is idolatry, for in worshiping money it is not worshiping money itself but worshiping the created things behind money. In order to obtain a commodity, men can use common currency to purchase it. This indicates how men want the things of God but not God himself. This is also why, except for those men who serve God, all other men serve Mammon (Matt. 6.24). Those who love money can never love God.

God's things come from God. So far as He is concerned, the created things which come from Him are not at all for sale. For all is grace. The sunlight, for example, cannot be measured, and it need not be paid for—since He causes it to shine on the unrighteous as well as on the righteous: His grace even causes the rain to fall on them both, without cost to anyone (Matt. 5.45). But electric lights and bottled water must be paid for. If men want to obtain anything from Satan they shall have to purchase it. Even the husks the prodigal son longed to eat must be bought at a cost, though he was by now penniless and "no man gave [any husks] unto him" (Luke 15.14-16). Therefore, a person who truly wishes to see God must be delivered from the Power of Money, for if his thought turns to it, he ceases to serve God. Oh how wrong it is to view all things in terms of money. But oh how right it is to look at all things from God's gracious perspective.

4 | Voluntary Poverty*

Matthew 6 tells us that "if . . . thine eye be single, thy whole body shall be full of light" (v.22). Our eye needs to be singly focused. Having said this, the Lord then mentions the matter of service. In serving the Lord, we must also be singly focused: "No man can serve two masters; . . . Ye cannot serve God and mammon" (v.24). The eye must be single, and service must be single. To serve Mammon is an awful bondage. He who wants to serve God must be delivered from it; otherwise he cannot serve God.

A single eye is an eye that is delivered from the idolatry of Mammon. Such singleness of eye enables us to see the truth. Truth is absolute and not relative. It is therefore not affected by anything. The reason why one fails to know God is because his eye is double-focused. To know Him it requires an eye that is freed from double vision. The double-visioned cannot see the truth. Such a person cannot see God.

*Delivered at Hardoon Road, Shanghai, 28 April 1948. —*Translator*

A Christian should look upon mammon or money as being a very harmful thing. He needs to let go of it quickly as though he were casting out of his hand a red hot coal. Christian poverty is something voluntarily taken up. Some are poor due to their environment. Others are poor through lack of inheritance or because of some unusual event. But some become poor voluntarily after they have experienced salvation. There is a vast difference between these two types of poverty. It can be likened to the difference between soldiers who become so by conscription and those who become so by volunteering.

Why voluntary poverty? Because the Bible declares that "it is hard for a rich man to enter into the kingdom of heaven. . . . It is easier for a camel to go through a needle's eye, than for a rich man to enter into the kingdom of God" (Matt. 19.23-24).

Mammon is equivalent to an idol. We are told by Scripture that a covetous man is an idolater (Eph. 5.5, Col. 3.5). Mammon represents wealth, riches, possessions, money. It all belongs to Caesar.

During the apostolic time the disciples had forsaken all to follow the Lord. We learn from Church history that tens of thousands of those who became followers of Francis of Assisi—later known as the Franciscans—had taken the vow of poverty as Francis had done. In this matter of voluntary poverty we are naturally overcautious. We are afraid of overdoing it. Count von Zinzendorf, the founder of the Moravian movement, was a highly educated man. He placed all his wealth on the sacrificial altar for the sake of the Lord. During the past several hundred years these

Moravians have sent out far more missionaries than have the other denominations. The Brethren in England have never liked to advertise themselves, but we have learned that many among them became poor voluntarily.

From the Old Testament we learn that when Rachel left Laban, she stole his teraphim, that is, the household idols. Such action was of course condemned (Gen. 31.32). Today Christians should deal with money and possessions as though dealing with an idol. Because a Christian must not have any idol at home, he must therefore also not lay up for himself any treasures upon the earth that become as it were an idol (see Matt. 6.19 again). Today the challenge for the Church is great in at least three areas: first, the need in the work; second, the need of poor brethren; and third, the constant need of the earthly poor in general. The word of the Lord is this: that "ye have the poor always with you" (Matt. 26.11). And consequently, we should take care of their needs.

Mammon is much more serious an issue than just having an idol. When the Church is strong it can stand on the ground of voluntary poverty. And thus, false brethren dare not come to the church because as soon as they enter into her midst they have to give themselves up. All who live by their eloquence, mind and cleverness are not able to remain in the church when the latter is strong by standing on the ground of voluntary poverty. Consequently, the church is kept clean. As money goes out, self is delivered. So if you wish to be clean, let money go out from you.

From the Biblical record we learn that our Lord had contact twice with money. The first instance involved the collection of the temple tax (Matt. 17.24-27). We realize from this event that our Lord had no money in His pocket. The second instance involved His entrusting into the care of Judas His and His disciples' money bag (John 12.6, 13.29). Again we learn that He had no money in His own pocket. Judas was a person most suited for touching money.

The principle which Paul enunciated is this (and in so doing he quoted from the Old Testament incident of the Israelites collecting the manna in the wilderness): "He that gathered much had nothing over; and he that gathered little had no lack" (2 Cor. 8.15). This, it may be said, is pertinent to the coordination in the Lord's work. In the body of Christ, if in gathering much there is something left over and if in gathering less there is a lack, then such an outcome bespeaks the absence of coordination.

Today in this matter of offering, it is not a question of one-tenth or two-tenths. It is a giving of everything beyond one's necessary personal requirements. Any consecration less than this is below the Lord's standard. All who serve must forsake everything and follow the Lord. Apart from personal daily needs, the rest should be given away. He who lays up treasures on the earth is he who serves Mammon.

Look at all the procedures people must go through in serving idols: the need to kneel, to burn incense, and so forth. Serving Mammon too is very complicated. Jesus in the Gospel of Matthew declared: "where thy treasure is, there will thy heart be also" (6.21). Preceding this is His word about laying up treasures in heaven or on earth. May our hearts be delivered from earthly treasures.

Today some are under the bondage of the world. But the bondage of money is much tighter than that of the world. Why give to the poor? Well, it is not just for the poor; even more so, perhaps, it is for you to be delivered from the power of Mammon. And by so doing, you may resolve the money issue in your life earlier. Some may think that giving to the poor is exclusively for the sake of them. Yes, indeed, the poor may be saved through your giving; yet even should the poor not be saved, you yourself shall reap a huge benefit. This is because the one who is willing to spend his money for others will be welcomed in heaven by many, whereas the one in whose life money is so central will have no one thanking him when he enters eternity. Let us spend and be spent for the Lord. And voluntary poverty is one of the ways to do so. Such is the kind of poverty about which Paul said this: "as poor, yet making many rich" (2 Cor. 6.10).

PART SIX

NEW TESTAMENT MINISTRY

1 | The Treasure in the Earthen Vessel*

The ministry spoken of in 2 Corinthians 3 is that of the New Covenant. The nature of New Covenant ministry is different from that of the Old Covenant. The focal point of this New Covenant ministry is expressed in 3.18 which reads: "with unveiled face beholding as a mirror the glory of the Lord."

2 Corinthians 4 tells us what is the consequence of having this kind of ministry. It also goes further to describe the relationship between the Lord and us. This relationship is defined in 4.7, where Paul declares: "we have this treasure in earthen vessels." This is a very important verse in the New Testament. The reason why ministry is laid upon us today is because we have this treasure in earthen vessels. Our outside is likened to an earthen vessel, the inside to the treasure. We do not merely give the treasure to men, we give them the treasure that is to be found in *earthen* vessels.

---

*Delivered at Hardoon Road, Shanghai, 17 April 1948. —*Translator*

Today's problem lies in our desire to beautify the earthen vessels instead of manifesting the treasure in the earthen vessels. Some hold on to themselves so tightly that the treasure is unable to break through. The principle of spiritual life is summed up in the phrase, the treasure in the earthen vessel. We are not to mend the earthen vessel nor change the natural man by any human method. Let us not labor to the extent that the vessel is no longer an *earthen* vessel. It is not because one does not say anything, hear anything and do anything that he or she is spiritual. An earthen vessel is always an earthen vessel. It is forever worth little. If the Lord so arranges that you be a student, then be that. If the Lord appoints you to be a housewife, then be content to be such. Your being a student or a housewife should not hide the treasure that is in you. The New Covenant ministry rests on how much treasure the Lord gives and not on how cleanly you wash or beautify your earthen vessel.

Today man is not innocent enough before God. He does additional work on the earthen vessel. But no matter how much work is done on his earthen vessel, the one and only result of such work will be to draw people's attention to himself. The ministry of Paul was manifested most wonderfully, yet his bodily presence was quite weak (2 Cor. 10.10). Today, however, man's ministry is weak but his personal appearance is fairly strong and attractive. How we need to go before God and learn the lesson of being smitten and dealt with. Our present need is not more outward human mending efforts. Our need instead is for people to be able to distinguish the inside treasure from the outside earthen vessel.

Miss Margaret Barber was one who truly waited for the Lord's second coming. She waited daily and yearly for the Lord to return. When people came into her presence, they saw Christ. One day I was in her study and noticed that her waste basket was full of discarded papers. She told me that she had started to write a letter in the morning, but before she finished it, she felt uneasy within herself. So she threw it away. She continued to discard her writing paper till the basket was full. And the letter was still unfinished. This demonstrates how she lived before the Lord.

Outward piety does not help in making a good Christian. Only that which the Lord has wrought in you is accounted as worthwhile. It is futile in attempting to be a Christian outwardly. All such efforts must be discarded. It is inward and not outward learning which makes a Christian. 2 Corinthians 4 mentions the dying or the slaying of Jesus (v.10). This slaying or "deathizing" occurs inwardly, not outwardly, in the life of the Christian. And it goes on *continuously.*

Let us not lead the brothers and sisters astray. Let us not teach people to speak and work like certain so-called saints. Such guidance is useless in the knowledge of God. If the counterfeit is present, the real will not come forth. If human effort remains, that which emanates from God will not come forth. The false must go before the real can come. Today the greatest principle to grasp hold of is this—the treasure in the earthen vessel. Let us not ever spend time in beautifying ourselves. It is wrong to indulge ourselves; it is equally wrong to decorate ourselves. God has no desire to adorn our earthen vessels. His thought is to cause the treasure to shine through such vessels.

Many do not realize how much pretension and make-believe they put up before men. During Christmas time one year, brother T. Austin-Sparks lay on the grass and played with his son and his dog. Such a scene was totally natural and beautiful. But many seem to have had their earthen vessels burnt by fire. In meeting them people feel as though there is something unnatural and even frightening about them. They pretend to such a degree that even their voice and speech seem to change before men. Such outward dissimulation is altogether useless.

The salvation of the Lord is in manifesting Christ before men, in presenting to them the Lord who is within us. We are not to draw people's attention to the earthen vessels. If we do, the one who is hurt most will be ourselves. No, we are to draw people to notice the Christ within us, for He is the treasure. "The Son of man came eating and drinking" (Matt. 11.19); but today's rule for some of us seems to be to neither eat nor drink. By being a little unnatural, strange or somewhat mysterious, we think we become spiritual. Yet we read in the Scriptures that "a prophet is not without honor, save in his own country, and in his own house" (Matt. 13.54-58). This is because in his native land all know a prophet's kith and kin. Hence, there is nothing mysterious about him.

True ministry is inward. Though a person may

receive the deepest work of God in his life, that person can still be readily approachable by other people. Evan Hopkins was the theologian of the Keswick movement. He preached especially on consecration and sanctification. He had a marvelous gift of drawing rabbits' ears. He frequently drew all kinds of rabbit ears to amuse his children and grandchildren. In the eyes of men, he may not have appeared spiritual. But God used him mightily to preach the word of holiness. God has not sent angels to preach holiness; instead, He uses ordinary men to do the preaching. In the Gospels we read how the Lord instructed the disciples to become as little children (see Matt. 18.3, Mark 10.15, Luke 18.17). Little children are not pretentious. Let us never pretend to be what we are not.

Natural innocency is quite different from spiritual innocency. The more we truly know Christ the simpler we become. Human ways will only make us more complicated. A carnal man has little inside. In fact, what he has outside is far more than that which he has inside. And because he has so little inside, he puts up a formidable facade. This is self-deceiving. A big brain or a strong emotion is nothing unless the one or the other is added to a strong and solid spirit.

Man's head occupies one-seventh of his entire body. If his head were to occupy one-third of his body, he would look very ugly. The same is true in the spiritual realm. Someone may have a good mind; yet if his thought becomes too strong and opinionated, he will not look good to others. But if it is joined to a strong spirit, the person turns out fine. The member of our physical body which projects itself the most is the nose. If a person bumps into a wall, his nose strikes it first. The strongest part of our inner being should be our spirit. We should have a good, strong and disciplined spirit so that when people touch us they will touch our spirit first and foremost. If what they touch instead is our learning or temperament, we fail in spiritual ministry.

2 | Brokenness and Ministry*

What is the relationship between knowing life and our service to God? "Knowing" cannot fully represent our way. Whether or not a person's ministry is released is dependent not only upon his knowing life but also upon his outward man being broken. The content of ministry is inner life.

Man has his inner as well as outer man. When the outward man is broken, his ministry can be discharged. In such a person, the deep calls unto the deep (Ps. 42.7). But in the person whose outer man remains unbroken, it will probably be that the shallow calls unto the shallow!

What we need today is the breaking of the outer man. Without such breaking, the inner man cannot be liberated. All which belongs to the outward needs to be broken; otherwise, the inward cannot be released. The earthen vessel must be broken before the inner treasure can show forth its power (2 Cor. 4.7).

*Delivered at Hardoon Road, Shanghai, 30 April 1948. —*Translator*

So long as the pure nard remains in the alabaster cruse, the odor of the ointment will not fill the house. But if the cruse be broken, the fragrance in profusion comes forth (John 12.3).

God deals with us daily through our circumstances. He works within us on the one hand and arranges our circumstances on the other. Strictly speaking, there is no such thing as chance in the life of a Christian since he has only the discipline of the Holy Spirit. For the Christian, all circumstances are the discipline of the Spirit. And the purpose of such discipline is to break the various elements of our outward man. As a man's reasoning is broken, his inner man flows out. As his emotion is also broken, his inner man issues forth.

Do not think that all is right so long as the words spoken are correct and properly delivered. No, there has to be another consideration here, and that is, whether these words are spoken outwardly or inwardly. An unbroken man may use the same vocabulary, utter the same word, even convey the same meaning as would the broken man but you cannot touch anything in what he has said. In order to be of service to God our outer man must be broken, for only then can our inner man be released. As our inner man comes forth, it touches the inner man of others.

A person who is clever in thinking and planning will be of little usefulness in spiritual things. You may say something laughingly or say it tearfully; yet the issue is not in how you say it but in how much of your inner man is released in the saying of it. To the extent a person is broken to that extent will be the measure of his ministry. How we need to have dealings before God in all these areas of our life. How we love to meet a person whose outward man has been wounded. For in meeting him we touch his inward man. The purpose of God's discipline is for the breaking of the outward man. A person may tell a woeful story on the platform without his being sorrowful himself. Or he may tell a joke without his being joyful at all. Such a person can act in theater but not preach God's word. Or the person whom you speak to can be so hard outwardly that he gives no response to whatever you may say. He can be likened to the people at the time of John the Baptist: "We piped unto you, and ye did not dance; we wailed, and ye did not mourn" (Matt. 11.17).

The basis of ministry is one's knowledge of God; but whether a person's ministry is effective or not depends on the breaking of his outer shell. If we wish to learn to be ministers of God's word, let us have this very understanding before God. More and more we shall find that without the wounding of the outer man, there can be no real ministry. I would again liken it to a rubber tree that will not yield its inner sap without a knife wound having been inflicted upon it. People without wounds cannot have ministry. Indeed there is no shortcut to ministry.

Let us never forget that whether or not one has a ministry depends on the dealing of the Lord's hand. If a person's spirit is unable to launch out, it is entirely because of his not being dealt with by the Lord. Then, too, whether his spirit is clean or not is also dependent upon God's dealing. But upon being dealt with, his spirit will become relatively clean.

As the outward man is broken, the inward man is released, and his word can touch others' hearts. Many think that so long as one can bring in an emotional atmosphere and stir up great enthusiasm it is an acceptable ministry. But without the outer man being wounded, a person does not have much real use. Christian service is based on brokenness. The degree of brokenness and wounds determine the degree of the Spirit's release.

How can one speak and have his spirit released? The one and only way is to have the outer shell dealt with. Its wholeness or brokenness decides the retaining or the releasing of man's inner spirit. For a person to have a usable spirit his outward man must be stricken. At our regeneration the Lord came into our spirit. As a result, our spirit became like the holiest of all in the tabernacle and temple of old—full of light and life. But whether the Lord is able to come forth depends on the brokenness of our outward man. But with it broken, all outward components will be outlets instead of hindrances. For instance, our mind and our emotion that have been broken (yet not destroyed) will no longer block the flow of life but will become instead the channels for the inner man to come forth. The dealt-with broken mind and emotion will turn out to be gates for the inner man. Today, whether or not Christ can be manifested through us hinges on whether or not we have been wounded and dealt with.

As was noted earlier, the nose is the most forward

part of the human body. If a person bumps into a wall, his nose will strike it first. What touches people first and foremost is a person's strongest and most prominent point. It can be his cleverness or his thought or his speech. For him to be able to serve the Lord, his strongest part will need to be wounded. And thus, his inner man can be released. How can we be unchanged and remain intact after we have believed the Lord for so many years?

You may say that you do not have great revelation from the Lord, but you cannot say that in so many years you have never experienced the discipline of the Holy Spirit. The purpose of His discipline is to make you a broken person. One day as you receive mercy from God, you may say, Now I understand what is meant to be a broken man. At that very time you will see how easy it is for your spirit to be released, once you have been severely dealt with and broken. The undisciplined believer provides the Lord with no outlet.

All spiritual things are given to the person who has become just right. The too diligent or the too lazy seeker will not find them. In our asking, we must ask just right, neither asking too much or too little. Here we need God's mercy. Growth will not come to him who runs nor to him who stands still. Only by God's mercy will you run or stand still in just the right way. For this reason, each one must commit himself to the God of all mercies (Rom 9.16).

Today, in fact, all we can say is that we have received God's mercy. Spiritual growth is beyond the ability of human energy. God will place us in a posi-

tion of utter powerlessness and impossibleness so
that He may have His way with us. If the Lord shows
His mercies to me, I will be carried through. But if
He does not show His mercies, there is nothing I can
do. Some are frequently thrashed in God's dealing of
them, yet their outer man seems never to be broken.
For us to be a minister, we can only appeal to God to
show His mercy.

We come to know the Lord through being
stricken and dealt with by Him. It is in the process of
being smitten that we learn to know Him. And as our
daily knowledge of the Lord is increased by the daily
blows upon our outward man, we are able to see how
the life of the Lord substitutes our life. Yet this is not
the increase of *life* but the increase of *knowledge*. For
this life we already have; only through the Lord's
dealings do we come to have a deeper *understanding*
of this life.

The spiritual life all believers possess is very rich
indeed, but we are ignorant of just how rich this life
actually is. Only at the time when our natural shell is
being broken do we realize how rich the life of the
Lord is: how it enables us to do the impossible!

During the First World War one man was hit by
forty-seven bullets and still remained alive. Here was
a human being who was able to take forty-seven hits
and survive. But if this body of ours has never been
wounded even once, how much it can endure cannot
be proven or determined. Now the riches of the
Lord's life are beyond our comprehension. For this
reason, therefore, no one should be grieved because
of trial, since trials not only test our faith but enable

us to manifest the life of the Lord. All which God has arranged for us to pass through is profitable to us in causing us to know Him. Only the tested know God, and only in knowing God can anyone serve Him.

Today we should commit ourselves wholly to the Lord's hand that He may do the necessary work in us. Unless we are so committed, He can do nothing. Formerly, there was a sister who quarreled with her family and threatened to commit suicide. She said she would jump into the river, so committed she appeared to be to take her own life. But as she approached the river, her family—who had followed after her—noticed that she carefully lifted up her skirt. By this they knew that she had no intention of taking her life. She had failed in her commitment to die. Today unless we lay our all on the altar, there is no spiritual way ahead for us. How can we forge ahead if we worry about this, fear that, or are so careful and so concerned lest we be too drastic? We must be willing to pay the cost. Let us be thorough and absolute in being Christian.

Today we are in the last days. We need to be violent with ourselves in the spirit of Matthew 11.12, or else there is no spiritual future. The halfhearted and double-minded cannot forge ahead. May there be absolute people among us who can provide the Lord with a highway on which to move forward.

PART SEVEN

APPENDIX

1 | The Relationship between Church and Work*

The Church Is Local, the Work Is Regional

The Church takes locality as its boundary, but the work takes region as its sphere of responsibility. A church is local, such as the church in Ephesus, the church in Colosse, and the church in Corinth. But the work extends beyond a locality. The Book of Acts shows us that the first group of workers began their work in Jerusalem, and went from Jerusalem to Samaria and to many other localities. In other words, these workers were not confined to Jerusalem but traveled freely throughout all Judea. Their work was regional in nature. Such were the beginnings at Jerusalem.

At Antioch there was a new beginning. There we see how Barnabas and Paul went forth to pioneer the work among the Gentiles. These Gentile lands included the local churches in Galatia and the local

---

*Delivered at Hardoon Road, Shanghai, 15 May 1948. —*Translator*

churches in Asia Minor, thus indicating that the work was regional. So in the Bible we see that there were not only Peter and his colleagues preaching the gospel, there were also Barnabas and his company preaching the gospel. And according to the Letter to the Philippians, there were still other groups of people preaching (1.15-17) in additional regions. The apostle Paul explained it this way: "according to the measure of the province which God appointed to us as a measure, to reach even unto you" (2 Cor. 10.13). In other words, Paul had his province or sphere of work.

So the work was regional, with each region including in its sphere several localities. Under normal conditions, and in spite of regional differences, there was still unity. All these different regions belonged to one fellowship. Jerusalem and Antioch were joined in one. Though their regions were different, they had fellowship in the Lord. When people got saved in Antioch, Jerusalem sent Barnabas out to visit them (Acts 11.20-28). Antioch came out of Jerusalem and it also returned to Jerusalem; for when Jerusalem was in need, Antioch sent the offering of the Gentile brethren to Jerusalem (11.27-29). Barnabas came from Jerusalem to Antioch (v.22), and Paul returned to Jerusalem from Antioch (15.2). Thus are we shown that even though the regions were different, they all belonged to one fellowship.

The responsibility of the elders is unto the local assembly where they are (Titus 1.5), whereas that of the apostles is unto the regional work. Peter and his fellow workers took care of the works that were undertaken in various localities in Judea, while Paul and his company took care of the work in Antioch and other Gentile places. The apostles worked within the boundary of the provinces or spheres which God had appointed to them (2 Cor. 10.13-14).

Two Meanings of "Church" in the New Testament

The word church in the New Testament has two distinct meanings: first, it has reference to the Universal Church (Matt. 16.18), and second, to the local church (18.17). The Universal Church is the General Church which includes all the churches past, present and future. The local church is the church in a given locality.

As to the Universal Church, there are two aspects: one, it is the Church that includes all the children of God—past, present and future. But besides this aspect, it also has reference to the sum total of all the children of God who today are living. For today we live neither in the past nor in the future. The past is gone, and the future is yet to come. In between the past and the future are all the children of God who are today living on earth. As children of God, we need to learn to be one with all the other children of God on earth as well as to be one with all the saints in the local assembly where we are (1 Cor. 11.16). In case there is controversy between the church in Nanking and the church in Shanghai, you may say they have only maintained the testimony of their own locality, they have not maintained God's testimony on earth. Today we must maintain not only the testimony of the locality but also the testimony of God on earth. We cannot be exclusive in keeping ourselves intact, because Shanghai belongs to the General Church on earth. The "body" in view in 1 Corinthians is different from the "body" in view in Ephesians 4. For the body in Ephesians 4 includes all believers past and present, whereas the body in 1 Corinthians refers to all the believers who were on earth at that particular time.

Because the church is local and the work is regional, a local church cannot contain a regional work, since a region is geographically larger than a local church. In practicing the unity of the Church, let us learn to practice well the unity of the General Church.

2 | Matters for Workers to Observe in Travel*

A worker should pay attention to several matters during his travels for the Lord.

The first of these concerns his relationship with the brethren at his destination points. When a worker arrives at a new place he must be careful in his relationship with the brothers and sisters there. Oftentimes such relationship may not be spiritual. The closeness or remoteness of our relationship with them is to be determined by spiritual circumstances. Here is an area of concern in which workers with a strong or weak personality need some special counsel. What follows may be helpful.

We should all be delivered from maintaining any sentimental relationship. Such a relationship is probably forged on the basis of similarity in temperament or position. Some workers have a close relationship with various people simply because their temperaments agree. Others have a special burden for some

---

*Delivered at Hardoon Road, Shanghai, 25 April 1948. —*Translator*

particular brother or sister because their weakness happens to be the same as theirs. Thus they become especially close to one another sentimentally. However, such relationships render no spiritual help to those in need; and consequently, many brothers and sisters are not blessed. All such sentimental relationships must be broken off. For any relationship we workers establish is to be spiritually based and not forged out of any sentimental consideration such as same temperament, same school, or same village.

Moreover, if we are in fellowship with a weak brother, we need to be most careful lest in trying to help him we ourselves fall into his condition (see Gal. 6.1). We should raise him to a higher level.

A second matter to be observed is for the Lord's workers to learn to condescend to the lowly. We must be careful of those who have fame, wealth or position in society. We need to keep a little distance from them to avoid any suspicion. Not everyone of God's servants may go to the house of a wealthy brother or sister. Let us not stay in the house of the wealthy. Sadly, today's Christianity and capitalism have merged into one. This has not been a good development.

Once when I was sick in Chefoo the brethren there asked me to stay with a well-to-do family, which I refused to do. They asked me why. My answer was that this had something to do with my walk before the Lord. Another time I had meetings in Kaifeng. At first I stayed in the house of a brother with a high social standing, but later I did not want to stay in such a high official's home. He who loves to gather with the wealthy or with those of high social status loses the dignity of a servant of God. I have no patience with such workers for they have forfeited their dignity.

As God's workmen we need to maintain the dignity of the ministers. Whether it was the Lord or the apostles, all seemed to have leveled a stronger reprimand against the wealthy and the high class. Unless in our walk before the Lord we have settled this issue of money, wealth and Mammon, we shall never exude the right fragrance.

In carrying on fellowship with other people, we should periodically take note as to whether or not our position on this issue has changed. Selective social intercourse is a shameful thing for a worker to engage in.

A third matter to be noticed by all God's workmen is unquestionably a considerable demand—which is, that we all must learn to listen. The fundamental requirement, skill and qualification of a worker is that he have the ability to hear. One should be able to sit for an hour listening to the brothers and sisters, and hearing every word. Not only must he hear what another says, he must also *understand* what is said. Only then can he speak a word of help to those in need.

As brothers and sisters are talking to us, we workers need to be quiet inwardly; that is to say, we do not speak within ourselves. Many hear wrongly because as they listen outwardly they also speak inwardly. This is like having two radios blasting out messages from two different stations. How can anyone hear clearly?!?

Another point in this same area of concern is that a man's spirit comes forth through his mouth. As people speak, their spirits are released so as to touch the spirits of other people. How can a person touch another's spirit if at the outset he does not know how to listen? A worker must listen before he can speak to the one in need.

A fourth matter to be observed by any workman for God is for him to learn to speak accurately during ordinary days at home. A careless person is hopeless in the work of God. The double-tongued can only work trouble but never render help in any local assembly. A brother once asked me how to study the Bible. Let me tell you, only an exact and careful person can study the Bible and get light from it. Some people by their very nature cannot study the Scriptures. It would be useless for them even if they were sent off to seminary. Some may be able to study philosophy but not science, for science is exact. Its knowledge has to pass through many experiments and proofs. As in science so in the work of the Lord, there is no such thing as "almost." It is either "yea, yea" or "nay, nay" (cf. 2 Cor. 1.17ff.). For example, the whiteness of snow and the whiteness of a horse are different. But to the careless person, they will be deemed to be the same. Hence in the work of the Lord we must be careful, exact and accurate in our speaking.

Let the sisters who serve the Lord pay particular attention to this matter. Let them be careful in their daily affairs, speaking precisely and circumspectly. God has not much use for the careless, the undiscerning and the overly active-minded. It takes effort to speak accurately, whereas it is more convenient to talk loosely. Yet the careless worker can only speak emotionally, not exactly. Nevertheless, truth, as we have said before, is absolute and is not subject to change by emotion. As a matter of fact, truth is not affected by any circumstance.

A fifth matter to be observed in a worker's travels for the Lord concerns the appointment of responsible brothers. Not every worker can appoint elders. Paul asked Timothy and Titus to set up elders, but apparently he did not call Mark, Silas, Luke, Demas, and others to do so. Some of us are to be hands, but not eyes. Think of yourself for a moment as a hand. Can a hand after much consideration determine whether a pillar is white? Even if it were to deliberate for five days, it could never figure out the color. It would have to ask the eye to see and determine. Those of us who are hands or ears but not eyes, let us be mindful of the fact that it is easy to set up a responsible brother, but it will be most troublesome to ask him to step down because of our own carelessness in having appointed him. How the entire Church suffers greatly in this respect. For this reason, we must not appoint responsible brothers carelessly. Paul called Timothy to seek for the faithful ones. This indeed is not a light area of concern.

A sixth matter to be discussed relates especially to the physical needs of the traveling worker. *As to personal living*, the basic principle to follow is to be light in luggage while traveling. It gives a bad impression if he carries much luggage. *And as to eating*, God's servant should eat whatever is put before him. Apart from special bodily weakness, he should be a person who is easily served. At home the worker can do whatever he wills, but in traveling outside he should not be so careless.

Once I went to Anhwai. The people there loved sesame oil, whereas for me I dreaded it. Yet I partook of the sesame oil during the sixteen days I was there. They noticed that I ate little. So they asked if I liked century-old eggs. I said yes. But when the eggs were served, they were floating in sesame oil!

Then as to dwelling. Workers should not choose too good or too bad a place to live. Find a place in between these extremes. Once the choice is made, stay there till departure. Even if you should end up living in a lion's den, you must stay till daybreak, for you cannot go out before the king arrives (see Dan. 6.19ff.). Unless there is another arrangement made for you, you should not move around. Many workers cause trouble because they move about staying in various dwelling places.

Once I was given a bed that was made up of small blocks. I could not lie down, for if I turned, the bed would make noises. Though I was afraid of noises from other people, I was even more fearful of making noises myself. A worker must learn how to abound and how to be abased (Phil. 4.12). Whenever and wherever he goes, he needs to bring his body under control.

There was a brother in southern Fukien. His living standard was comparatively high. Moreover, he was unable to adjust himself to serve the Lord in places where the living standard was lower than his. Let us ever be mindful that though what we eat and are clothed in and live in at home is a personal matter before God, when we are in another's house we need to live in accordance with the living standard of that house. Personal habit and convenience is one thing; the will to suffer in relation to circumstances with others is another. No matter how weak or how necessary our physical bodies are, we still must learn to abase ourselves. Do not let a local assembly elsewhere feel the burden of entertaining a servant of the Lord. If we as God's workmen learn to live lowly in our own home, we will be able to endure when we are placed in a still lower place. Only the one who has learned to put his body in subjection gives no trouble to other people. The will to suffer can alone give us strength to abase ourselves before men. Hence we must bring our bodies into subjection so that we can learn how to be abased when required.

We should also know how to abound. But *knowing* abundance is not the same as *enjoying* abundance. I must know how to eat and how not to eat. A gluttonous person reveals that he has never been disciplined before God. If I need a chicken daily, I can daily eat one. But if I have no such need, then I will not eat even if five chickens are set before me. I eat within my portion.

Satan's sin was lusting after the throne (Is. 14.13-14). Man sinned through the lust of eating (Gen. 3.6). It is not a matter of eating more or eating less. Whatever is put before us we may eat. Whatever is given we accept without asking for more. Whenever I am among people I have to maintain my position as a servant of the Lord; otherwise, it will give the gospel a bad impression. On one occasion, before many young people went out to work I invited them for a meal. Their conduct at this meal was the deciding factor as to whether anyone of them could go out to the work or not. Now that I have mentioned this, perhaps I will not be able to invite anyone to a meal next time!

Finally, regarding the matter of receiving gifts while traveling in the work of the Lord. Let me tell you a story. In 1937 I was in Manila. Upon departing, the brothers and sisters there presented me with a box of fruits which amounted to between one hundred eighty and two hundred pieces. Had I put these up in my room on the ship, I could easily have opened a small fruit stand. But when I came off the ship, I had not one piece of fruit left. I had given them to the waiters on the ship. Though they were not poor, nevertheless they were poor in fruit. Had I brought those two hundred fruits home, what would people have thought? They would have wondered aloud how it was that a preacher of the gospel could have brought home so many things!

We are not able to give gifts in return to those who have gifted us. For there would be no end to such courtesy. We are not able to return the love of the brothers and sisters; yet we are able to share with the poor in love.